MISSISSIPPI

River Country Tales

A Celebration of 500 Years of Deep South History

JIM FRAISER

Foreword by
William F. Winter

PELICAN PUBLISHING COMPANY
Gretna 2001

*The word "Pelican" and the depiction of a pelican are trademarks
of Pelican Publishing Company, Inc., and are registered in the
U.S. Patent and Trademark Office.*

Library of Congress Cataloging-in-Publication

Fraiser, Jim, 1954-
   Mississippi river country tales : a celebration of 500 years of Deep South history
/ Jim Fraiser.
     p. cm.
   Includes bibliographical references (p.).
   ISBN 1-56554-787-X (pbk. : alk. paper)
   1. Mississippi River Valley—History—Anecdotes. I. Title.

F351 .F82 2000
977—dc21

                                     00-035948

Photographs by Deborah Blakeney and Jim Fraiser

Printed in Canada

Published by Pelican Publishing Company, Inc.
1000 Burmaster Street, Gretna, Louisiana 70053

For my wife, Carole, and my daughters,
Lucy and Mary Adelyn

The river country's wide and flat
  And blurred ash-blue with the sun,
And there all work is dreams come true
  All dreams are work begun.
The silted river made for us
  The black and mellow soil
And taught us as we conquered him
  Courage, faith and toil.

—William Alexander Percy, from *In the Delta*

CONTENTS

FOREWORD

Growing up thirty years and thirty miles apart, Jim Fraiser and I share a common heritage and a common passion born of the river country of Mississippi about which he writes so well. I spent my boyhood along one of those rivers, the Yalobusha, which a few serpentine bends downstream meets the Tallahatchie at Fraiser's hometown of Greenwood, there to form the storied Yazoo. It was in this setting that he and I both developed an appreciation for and an understanding of the subjects of this book. This volume is written out of much that Fraiser personally knows about but, more than that, out of his deep feeling for the place that he calls home.

No one who has ever lived in this mystical region can fail to appreciate the incredible mother lode of material that Fraiser has tapped in presenting this compilation of stories from more than four centuries of history. Most of them have been told before in one form or another in separate accounts. Many of them have formed the basis of the writings of Faulkner, Twain, Welty, and so many other of the region's great literary figures.

Nowhere, however, so far as I am aware, has one author put together so diverse and comprehensive a collection of stories about the region and tied them together around its history and its rivers.

This volume should not be characterized as history, although it relates many of the historic events that have marked the region's past. What it really is about is the recounting of the human-interest stories that have made that history so fascinating. So many of them are the tales that have been told and retold around countless campfires of deer hunters deep in the Delta woods or by hundreds of courthouse raconteurs gathered on frosty mornings in hundreds of little coffee shops in communities across the region.

Each chapter of this narrative is adorned by the likes of Pinckney Pinchback, the freed son of a slave woman and a Mississippi plantation owner, who, after fighting as a Union officer in the Civil War, went on to become the first black governor of Louisiana. He was just one of a never-ending succession of colorful heroes and scoundrels, ministers and minstrels, brawlers, buffoons, and community builders who combined to create one of the most fascinating places on the face of the earth.

These incredible characters were real people who bore names like Machine Gun Kelly and Wild Bill Sullivan, Muddy Waters and Howlin' Wolf, Abe Huffstickler and Greenwood LeFlore, Theodore G. Bilbo and Fannie Lou Hamer. They ran the gamut of personalities from those reflecting the basest and meanest prejudices to those exemplifying the highest ideals. This book in essence is about our forebears, our relatives, our neighbors, and ourselves. It is about how somehow, in spite of our foolishness and our mistakes, we wound up forming a pretty civilized society out of the raw river wilderness.

This volume further points out what so many people outside the region fail to understand about it, and that is its cultural variety. No other region of the country is richer in its racial diversity. Fraiser relates the invaluable contributions that have been made by people of all racial and ethnic backgrounds. He points out with rare perceptiveness the continuing impact of this intriguing mix of cultures on the region today.

Jim Fraiser's *Mississippi River Country Tales* is a well-researched, well-documented, well-assembled piece of work that is a highly attractive and valuable addition to the never-ending process of interpreting and understanding where we have come from, what we have inherited, and perhaps, most important of all, what values and lessons from our past we can apply to our own lives.

This book can do nothing but add to Jim Fraiser's growing reputation as another young Mississippi writer who knows how to tell stories about the places and people he knows best—about, in Faulkner's words, that "postage stamp" that for Fraiser is the river country of Mississippi. It is, as its subtitle suggests, a celebration of our history.

William F. Winter

ACKNOWLEDGMENTS

I am deeply indebted to the staff of the Mississippi Department of Archives, the Old Capitol Museum bookstore, the Eudora Welty Library, and the Mississippi State Law Library for their assistance to this project; to my wife, Carole, and my parents, Adelyn and John, for their editorial support; to Deborah Blakeney for her extraordinary vision; to Lucy and Mary Adelyn for endless inspiration; to my sister, Martha Bryant; and to my friends C. A. Dodson, John Clay, Greg Hardy, Wyatt Emmerich, Tim Kalich, Charles Wilson, Nina Kooij, Jimmy Cade, Gary Shute, Stephen Hogue, Missy Wyatt, and Terry Sullivan for their sage advice, which helped make this river-country dog hunt.

INTRODUCTION

Having spent over forty years in the Mississippi river country, I can personally attest to a sensation experienced by many of that region's inhabitants. It's called "nostertia," that peculiar blend of nostalgia and inertia created by a combination of the river country's sweltering heat and its citizens' unparalleled sense of place. While we've learned to endure our homeland's near tropical sultriness, we've come to treasure our renowned sense of Southern identity as surely as we do our other five senses. And though we recognize that most Americans get on quite well without so concrete a sense of identity as ours, we wouldn't trade our fabled sixth sense for all the network TV, fast-food restaurants, five-lane highways, and Internet access available to any forward-looking, twenty-first-century citizen. For, although we enjoy the aforesaid modern conveniences as much as other Americans, we Mississippi river-country folk also take pride in occasionally availing ourselves of something more of the soul than of science; something imbedded far deeper in our psyches than a Big Mac or TV sitcom could ever hope to penetrate.

Indeed, our Deep South sense of place could never have arisen in such epochs as history-starved seventeenth-century Idaho or technologically inundated twentieth-century California. It is precisely the extraordinary history of the Mississippi river country that bestows upon us our immutable feeling of being a part of something uncommon in all creation. And from the very beginning, for each passing generation of all races, nationalities, and creeds, there was the ubiquitous presence of the rivers that formed and enriched our region. These streams first presented themselves as obstacles to cross, then became in turn our highways of commerce, our marine battlegrounds, and finally, our beautiful but deadly reminders that the only thing constant about life is change.

My very first memory, acquired during my second year, is that of the seemingly boundless Mississippi River, viewed from a vantage alongside a New Orleans bridge. I've since marveled at the intrepidity of the riverboat men and women who made this inland ocean their home, and shuddered at the thought of my parents, as Delta refugees in the 1920s, running for their very lives when that stream proved to be unbounded by man's best efforts. Growing up with the Tallahatchie River as the northernmost boundary of my backyard, I often fantasized about taking part in the Civil War battle waged a few miles upriver at Fort Pemberton, and occasionally dove beneath that river's dark brown, silt-imbued surface in search of the *Star of the West*'s hull—the ship the Confederates used to slow General Grant's relentless drive to Vicksburg. Years later, my friends and I steered our johnboats past Point Leflore a few miles downriver, where, fifty years earlier, the great Choctaw chief and U.S. senator Greenwood LeFlore had established his own cotton port in hopes of making a ghost town of the city that would later bear his name.

Since moving from Greenwood to Jackson, I occasionally fish for bass, crappie, and bream in the Pearl River no more than a stone's throw from my Belhaven home. While gazing at the familiar kudzu, cross-vines, oaks, and Spanish-moss-draped cypress, I've wondered what prompted French-Canadian trader Louis LeFleur to abandon his lovely Pearl River environs in 1812 and set up shop on the Natchez Trace. A subsequent jaunt down the eerie Old Sunken Trace near Natchez, where land pirates ambushed and murdered early 1800s travelers, gave me no insights into that enduring mystery.

To belabor the obvious, our Mississippi river-country streams are as steeped in history and legend as they are in beauty. The Mississippi, Yazoo, Tallahatchie, Big Black, Tallahala, Biloxi, Pascagoula, Chickasawhay, Tombigbee, Deer Creek, Noxubee, Sunflower, Pearl, Leaf . . . these are the rivers that spawned such towns as Memphis, Greenville, Natchez, Vicksburg, Port Hudson, New Orleans, Clarksdale, Greenwood, Columbus, Yazoo City, Jackson, Laurel, Hattiesburg, Gulfport, Biloxi, and Ocean Springs. And these very cities were the stages upon which the famous—De Soto, La Salle, Iberville, Andrew Jackson, Pushmataha, Jim Bowie, L. Q. C. Lamar, Teddy Roosevelt, Greenwood LeFlore, Bedford Forrest, U. S. Grant, John L. Sullivan, William Faulkner, Mark Twain, Walter Anderson, Fannie Lou Hamer, Medgar Evers, Cool Papa Bell, Archie Manning, Walter Payton, Jimmy Rodgers, Robert Johnson, and many more—made their marks and met their fates. This region produced the infamous as well: Samuel Mason, Wiley Harpe, Newt Knight, Wild Bill Sullivan, Machine Gun Kelly, Theodore Bilbo, and James K. Vardaman. Here too was the immortal stuff of myth and legend: the missing Pascagoula River people, the Great Spirit in the Garden of Eden, a Tombigbee River ghost ship, a Yazoo City witch, the specters inhabiting King's Tavern, myriad haunted river-country mansions, the heroic Casey Jones, the larger-than-life Annie Christmas, the Devil at the Delta crossroads, and the infamous Stagolee. But the river country has also been home to many not-so-well-known folk who strove just as mightily as the famous to create, preserve, and glorify their river-country homeland, including the Boy Who Saved Vicksburg and the Girl the Mississippi River Couldn't Beat.

Their stories and many more, from the humorous to the momentous, grace these pages. There's the New World's first Mardi Gras, a foiled plot to overthrow the newly formed United States, a Mississippi county's secession from the Confederacy, the Deep South's greatest duels, plantations won in card games, the beginnings of country, rap, blues, jazz, and rock-and-roll music, some of America's greatest sports heroes, and a maritime disaster that took a greater human toll than did the *Titanic*'s.

More than reminding us who we are and where we came from, these tales are a testimonial to those brave and hardy souls who gave present-day Mississippi river-country denizens more than just a place to live. This is the story of the heroes, villains, and legendary characters who, through their courageous or cowardly acts, compassionate or malicious intentions, or inexhaustible sense of humor and spirit of adventure, left their progeny a sense of history that so permeates their daily existence as to leave them forever assured of their immutable place in an increasingly capricious world.

MISSISSIPPI
River Country Tales

Chapter One

OF CONQUISTADORS AND EXPLORERS

Consummating a journey more perilous than man's trip to the moon, the Spanish, French, and British discovered, settled, and then wrested the Mississippi River valley away from the local Indian tribes, including the Natchez, Choctaws, and Chickasaws. These intrepid European and Canadian adventurers, Navarez, De Soto, La Salle, Tonti, Bienville, Iberville, Dunbar, and LeFleur, made an indelible stamp upon river-country history, not only because their names appear so prominently on current American maps, but also because of their establishment of cotton plantations and use of an involuntary labor supply to harvest them, which forever altered America's destiny. Three of the greatest of these adventurers were the Spanish conquistador Hernando De Soto and the French-Canadian explorers and settlers, Pierre le Moyne d'Iberville and Louis LeFleur.

De Soto discovered the Mississippi River, suffered defeats by the Chickasaws and Natchez, and was buried in that stream. After Iberville founded Old Biloxi (Ocean Springs) and celebrated America's first Mardi Gras, he, too, suffered ignominious defeat at the natives' hands. LeFleur, who established a trading post that later became the site of Mississippi's capital city, became fast friends with the Choctaws, and lived a long, pleasant

La Pointe-Krebs House (1726), Pascagoula

life. LeFleur's success not only helped open the Mississippi river-country frontier, it also gave birth to the now-familiar Southern adage, "If'n you can't whup 'em, jine 'em!"

THE CONQUEROR CONQUERED

How often have you heard that yet another Yankee abandoned his homeland and ensconced himself in the sunny Southland only to tragically lose his heart, his mind, or his life in the pursuit of the South's most prized asset—the enigmatic Southern belle? The first of such incidents occurred in 1540, and the first victim was Don Hernando De Soto, self-proclaimed "Child of the Sun," Spanish knight, governor of Cuba, ravager of Florida, and all-day sucker for a pretty Southern face. In June 1539, De Soto landed at Tampa Bay with 514 men, 237 horses, two women, eight priests, numerous attack dogs, and hundreds of hogs. Although a wiser conqueror would have known that traversing both an ocean and a continent with 500 men and only two women was asking for trouble, the thirty-eight-year-old conquistador confidently headed west from Spain on a mission of God, gold, and glory. To the surprise of few others, he met with disappointment, disaster, and death.

Not that the treasure hunter was altogether lacking in prospects of pleasant, New World, feminine companionship. After all, the native men had never seen gleaming armor, death-dealing crossbows, or the horrifying European "fire sticks," and the native women were plentiful, exotic, and scantily clad. What's more, as De Soto's Portuguese chronicler rather disingenuously noted, "Because the Indians had not heard of the Christians, they were careless."

Under the direction of his guide and interpreter Juan Ortiz, a survivor of Pamphilo de Navarez's 1528 New World debacle, De Soto's march to the Mississippi was interrupted in the spring of 1540 by an introduction to one of the most beautiful women the South ever produced—a chieftainess of the Cafitachequi known only to the Spanish as "the Lady." Delicately clad in fine chamois, adorned with multicolored feathers, and draped in exquisite pearls, this teenaged beauty proved every inch the sophisticated, all-powerful queen of the jungle. But like so many of our comely Southern lasses, this Lady's charms were exceeded only by her shrewdness.

Quickly realizing that Spanish curiosity was best piqued by feminine reticence, the Lady met De Soto's requests for gold with offers of pearls, and answered his romantic approaches by playing hard to get. Then, when De Soto forced her to travel along with his band as hostage, she contrived to deprive him of her company altogether. Consigned to the strict surveillance of three African slaves, the Lady asked De Soto's permission to temporarily halt the march to answer the call of nature in wooded seclusion. After the conqueror noticed that she was late returning, a search revealed that the Lady and her three keepers had given the Spanish the slip.

A few days later, two of the slaves returned to the Spanish party with a surprising tale of romance. The Lady and the missing African had eloped, married, and returned to her village. The Indian Queen, it seemed, preferred to take a mate of her own choosing—one not nearly so wealthy and powerful as De Soto, but a man having enough sense to know that, more than all the riches in the world, Southern women desire the privilege, nay, their inalienable right, to live life on nothing less than their very own terms!

NEW WORLD COOKOUT

Despairing over the loss of his Lady, De Soto resumed his voyage, which, in the spring of 1541, led his charges across the Tombigbee River near present-day Columbus, and into the Mississippi river country. Shortly thereafter, their westward march led them to a Chickasaw village in what is now Tallahatchie County. These natives, reputed to be "very warlike and much dreaded," surprised De Soto with warm greetings and gifts of food. In return, the Spaniards treated the Chickasaws to their first taste of barbecued pork, which the Indians, like all native Southerners, found much to their liking. But when tribesmen were later caught stealing Spanish hogs, the Spaniards unceremoniously lopped off their hands. Although the Chickasaws accepted these punishments with only mild disdain, De Soto's subsequent demand for 200 of the "youngest and least ugly women" to travel with his men aroused their warlike inclinations.

Disguising their anger, the Chickasaws waited until nightfall, sneaked into the Spanish camp, and used flaming arrows and hot coals from clay pots to set the Spaniards' wooden huts on fire. They slaughtered soldiers stumbling out of their huts in their bedclothes until De Soto mounted his horse and gamely launched a one-man counterattack. This gave the Spaniards time to regroup and snatch victory from the jaws of defeat, but not before sustaining the loss of forty soldiers, sixty horses, and 300 hogs. The Spaniards limped away to their destiny, discovering the Mississippi River on May 8, 1541, in either present-day Tunica or Coahoma county. But their suffering at the hands of river-country natives was far from over.

In 1542, De Soto finally despaired of finding gold to the west and returned to the Mississippi. Desirous of crossing over into what would later become known as the Natchez District, he sent a scouting party to confirm reports that the region was particularly fertile and already well cultivated by the natives. After the scouts returned with news of a hostile sun-worshiping tribe, De Soto, weary of battle, his forces reduced by more than half, and bereft of the bulk of his supplies, decided to approach the Natchez Indians with guile instead of force. He sent a message to their chief that he and his men were Children of the Sun, hoping the natives would accept him as a god.

The chief was unimpressed, and added insult to injury by replying, "You say that you are the Child of the Sun, and if you would dry up the River I would believe you. All who visit me serve, obey, and pay me tributes willingly or by force. If you desire to see me, come on, and if you come in peace, I will receive you with good will. And if you come in war, I will give that here. Not for you or anyone else will I shrink back one foot!"

Not long thereafter, De Soto found his final resting place in the Mississippi's muddy waters near present-day Natchez, but not without having learned some hard lessons at the river-country natives' hands—don't tease Southerners with barbecue, don't insult their women at all, and don't let your prideful mouth overload your armor-clad rear end!

RETURN TO SENDER

On April 6, 1682, French explorer René Robert Cavelier, Sieur de la Salle, his gallant, Italian soldier of fortune, Henri de Tonti, and their band of French-Canadians claimed the mouth of the Mississippi River for the French Sun King, Louis XIV. They had ventured downriver from Canada seeking the mouth of De Soto's great river and, having found it, offered a solemn prayer of thanks and sang a rousing chorus of France's national anthem.

Five years later, La Salle was murdered by mutineers near present-day Natchez while en route from Fort St. Louis (in east Texas) to Canada. Growing alarmed when La Salle failed to arrive on schedule, Tonti returned downriver to the site of their great 1682 discovery to search for his friend. When he finally called off the search, Tonti left a message for La Salle with his Gulf Coast Indian friends. Twelve years later, when Iberville landed at Old Biloxi, the natives handed him Tonti's message, which read, "It gives me great uneasiness to be obliged to return under the misfortune of not having found you. Two canoes have examined the coast, thirty leagues toward Mexico and twenty-five toward Florida."

Tonti refused to allow La Salle's premature death to rob his friend of his rightful place in the history of New World exploration. In 1697, he published a lasting tribute to his commander entitled *La Salle's Last Discoveries in America.*

THROW ME A DOUBLOON, MISTER!

To jump-start the colonization of the part of the lower Mississippi River valley they called New France, old France sent Pierre le Moyne d'Iberville to North America on September 28, 1698. Finding the Spanish in control of Florida, Iberville sailed westward along the Gulf Coast until on February 10, 1699, he and his four ships, 100 soldiers, and 200 settlers anchored at Ship Island just off the coast near present-day Ocean Springs. Iberville named a nearby isle "Deer Island" for the abundant deer thereon, but mistakenly named another "Cat Island" for the racoons he discovered there, which Europeans had never before encountered and assumed to be cats.

During the first few days ashore, Iberville and his men set out to find the mouth of the "Myssysypy" River. The first rivers they encountered were the Biloxi and Pascagoula, named in honor of the friendly tribes residing on their banks. Landing their boats proved as dangerous as it was difficult, as Iberville's occasionally sarcastic February 1699 diary entries reveal: "It is a jolly business indeed to explore the sea coasts with longboats that are not big enough to keep to the sea either under sail or at anchor, and are too big to approach a flat coast on which they run aground and touch bottom a half a league off shore."

Although he and his men once killed fifty deer during a three-day hunting trip near present-day Bay St. Louis, Iberville found other native wildlife substantially more troublesome. On one occasion, he was forced to hurriedly break camp when he and his party were descended upon by "the small flies or cousins, which the Indians call Marangouins [mosquitoes], which puncture the skin very savagely."

The French were more fortunate in their native diplomacy, communicating with the Indians through sign language and offering them presents of axes, knives, shirts, tobacco, pipes, brandy, wine, and glass beads. Although the Biloxi and Pascagoula were impressed with these gifts, their interest in consuming brandy diminished significantly after the French displayed that liquor's exceptional capacity for combustion. Nevertheless, the Biloxi instituted a great tradition of Southern hospitality by offering a peace pipe (calumet) and treating the French to a feast of bison, deer, bear, oysters, watermelons, and pumpkins.

With their aid, Iberville founded North America's second-oldest settlement, at present-day Ocean Springs. Shortly thereafter, after receiving the natives' directions to the Mississippi, Iberville set out in a longboat to find the great river. Then, on March 3, 1699, from a longboat's bow in an inland bayou, Iberville celebrated the New World's first Mardi Gras, giving prayers of thanks and offering the celebrants a bottle of wine.

Mardi Gras was originally a Greek festival of spring, which later became the Roman pagan orgy, Bacchanalia. Never ones to miss out on a good time, especially where converts could be had in the bargain, the original Roman Catholics (in a spirit greatly akin to that of modern-day Southern Catholics) transformed that pagan festival into a religious ceremony called "carnevale," or "a farewell to the flesh." Mardi Gras is now celebrated in all Catholic lands, including France, Spain, Latin America, South Louisiana, and the Mississippi Gulf Coast.

Biloxi's first Mardi Gras parade was held in 1908, but the first Mardi Gras parade in the U.S. with floats, costumed riders, and flambeaux bearers took place in New Orleans on March 24, 1857. Since then, there has been no shortage of floats, costumes, wine, brandy, oysters, knives, tobacco (or other smoked herbs), beads (glass or plastic), and Dixie beer at Mardi Gras revelries from Ocean Springs to New Orleans.

MIRROR, MIRROR

Hopelessly outnumbered and entirely surrounded by potentially hostile tribes, French colonialists swiftly recognized the necessity of producing leaders capable of pacifying their native hosts. No one enjoyed more success in this regard than Henri de Tonti, explorer of the Mississippi, Pearl, Biloxi, Yazoo, and Tallahatchie rivers. Nicknamed "Iron Hand" because his right hand had been blown off by a grenade and replaced by an iron one, Tonti had a natural faculty for command and courage under fire and a self-evident sense of integrity that greatly impressed the native tribesmen.

But it was this nobleman's presence of mind that saved him from destruction at the

Indians' hands in December of 1699. With hostile savages preparing to take his life, Tonti declared that he was surprised that they would kill a man who always carried their images in his heart. He then threw open his shirt and exposed a mirror that showed the Indians their own reflections, thereby blunting their lust for Tonti's blood. After word spread among the natives about this incident, they forever viewed the "one-handed chief" as both a great warrior and a medicine man, someone doubly dangerous to offend. With continued courage and cunning, Tonti faithfully served the colony until his death of yellow fever at Old Biloxi (Ocean Springs) in 1704.

DON'T FORGET THE WOMEN!

Iberville began colonizing New France in 1700. One of his men, Joseph Simon de la Pointe, established a settlement in present-day Pascagoula, where one of his cypress- and juniper-forged buildings still stands, known today as the La Pointe-Krebs House, the South's oldest residential landmark. But in the Mississippi river country, a house is not considered a home until graced with a woman's touch, and the French had no desire to repeat De Soto's mistake of failing to bring a sufficient contingent of women for New World barbecue cookouts. Accordingly, they sent for their womenfolk as soon as they established a settlement on the Mississippi coast. In the summer of 1704, a year after Fort Maurepas had been completed at Old Biloxi, the good ship *Pelican* arrived with a priest, soldiers and supplies, and most importantly, twenty-three young women under the care of four Sisters of Charity.

Unlike the women of dubious reputation delivered to New Orleans some years later, these former French orphans had been certified by the French minister as having "irreproachable character." Known as "casket girls" for the small chests (caskets) in which they carried all their possessions, they were all married shortly upon arrival, and the colony's first child was born in October of 1705. Not surprisingly, the women found life so difficult in the Biloxi colony they started a "petticoat rebellion" a few years later. Even paradise, it must be noted, cannot guarantee a lengthy abeyance in the eternal War between the Sexes. And river-country folk wouldn't have it any other way!

I'M TOO SEXY FOR MY ARMOR

One of Iberville's captains during the 1699 coast exploration, Laurent de Graff, was a celebrated buccaneer who had gained the French an impressive victory at Vera Cruz in 1683. A contemporary's description of de Graff shows the extent to which the French were impressed with their own romantic reputation:

> Capt. De Graff was tall and straight; his countenance handsome, but not effeminate. His hair was of a golden blonde, and a mustache after the Spanish fashion that admirably became him. A better canonier was never known. He could tell exactly where a ball would strike when he directed the gun. He was prompt, bold and determined. To resolve, undertake and execute were to him too

Possible site of Iberville's landing at Old Biloxi (Ocean Springs), with reconstructed Fort Maurepas in background

much. He was perfectly intrepid in dangers, but impatient, passionate, and swore too much. . . . He was proficient in music, with a most melodious voice. Thus he distinguished himself by his politeness and tastes, no less than by his audacity. And wherever he went, crowds gathered around to satisfy themselves whether he was a man or a demi-god.

As anyone even remotely familiar with the French well knows, 300 years has done little to temper their arrogance. Nor has it cured their penchant for disaster whenever engaging in warfare with the peoples of both the Eastern and Western hemispheres. Even so, anyone with discerning taste buds can thank their lucky stars that the French, and not the British, first settled the Mississippi river country!

EENY, MEENY, MINEY, MO

The year 1718 was a momentous one for the burgeoning French colony. Its management was turned over to the India Company, which later proved a total disaster when John Law's Mississippi Company's bubble burst two years later, nearly bankrupting the French government. Colonial slave trading was instituted that year, with healthy male and female slaves selling for 680 livres ($176) apiece, half at purchase and the remainder due within a year. Also on the agenda was the crucial issue of which village should thereafter serve as the seat of colonial government—Biloxi, New Orleans, or Natchez.

Iberville's brother, Jean Baptiste Le Moyne, Sieur de Bienville, favored New Orleans' agricultural potential, but Commissary Gen. Hubert de St. Malo feared New Orleans' vulnerability to flooding and invasion from the north or south. He recommended Natchez as the seat of colonial power, because the bluff city was more picturesque, appeared safe from floods or hurricanes, was better fortified and less vulnerable from attack by land, river, or sea, was a couple of hundred miles closer to Canadian and Illinois trading posts, and offered the richest agricultural district in the colony. D'Epinay, the new colonial governor, preferred that the seat remain at New (present-day) Biloxi, despite the fact that, of the three choices, Biloxi was most subject to assault by land or sea, offered the worst farmland of the three settlements, was frequently drubbed by hurricanes, and was most distant from friendly Illinois trading posts.

Needless to say, the French stooges chose Biloxi, thereby hastening their colony's demise and depriving Natchez of its chance to become the Deep South's leading city. Nevertheless, no one fond of deep-sea fishing, world-class casino resorts, five-star seafood restaurants, and breathtaking golf courses has ever complained that D'Epinay's choice assured New Biloxi's survival!

CONSCIENCE NOIRE

In 1723 a terrible hurricane ravaged New Orleans, but Ship Island proved a surprisingly safe haven from the storm. Also that year, gambling was outlawed in the colony and Governor Bienville drafted the first of many statutes designed at least in part to deal with the colony's growing slave population. Fully instituted the next year, the *Code Noir,* or Black Code, expelled Jews from the colony, required slaves to be raised Catholic, prohibited Protestant worship, banned slave work on Sundays, provided for slave marriages, barred all slave transactions that split up married couples, and forbade interracial marriage. Never one to be accused of taking half-measures, Bienville also mandated the death penalty for anyone convicted of maiming or killing colonial horses or cattle!

THE NOT-SO-GREAT ESCAPE

Violence and cruelty were commonplace during the exploration, conquest, and settlement of the lower Mississippi River valley. Shortly after their arrival in the New World, the French marveled at the natives' penchant for brutality, often shuddering when observing native warfare and religious ceremonies in which men, women, and children were burned at the stake, tomahawked, or buried alive, respectively. Even Louisiana's capital city, Baton Rouge, took its name from a bend in the Mississippi River where the Houmas once planted a red stick to signify their victory over the Tunicas and to serve as a seventeenth-century No Trespassing sign to the vanquished. As it turned out, the French wasted little time hopping on the violent bandwagon.

They and the Natchez were particularly brutal toward each other, the Natchez disemboweling pregnant French women and slaying their unborn infants during the massacre of Fort Rosalie, and the French retaliating by entirely exterminating the Natchez tribe. The horrors only increased when the British arrived, with the Choctaws backing the French and the Chickasaws aiding the newcomers. Many a captured brave or soldier perished by fire, while others were consigned to the slave's existence.

But not all colonial-era cruelty occurred as the result of violence between opposing forces. In 1754 the French maintained a garrison on Cat Island just off present-day Gulfport. Duroux, the commander, was renowned for his cruelty, often punishing his charges by stripping them naked and exposing them to mosquitoes and sand flies all night. Finally fed up with their commandant's excesses, the soldiers murdered Duroux and escaped to the mainland in search of a British settlement. At the request of French governor Kerlerec, the Choctaws pursued and captured the rebels, and haled them to New Orleans in irons. There, in what is now called Jackson Square, two were broken on the wheel and a third was placed alive in a coffin and sawed in half. A colonial citizen, Baudrot, whom the mutineers had forced to serve as their guide through the swamps, was also tortured to death despite the mutineers' testimony that he had acted under their coercion!

It should come as no surprise that anyone capable of such horrors would establish and nurture the cruelest of institutions, that hell of interminable woe called human bondage.

BRITISH LABOR PARTY

Cotton was first harvested in Mississippi in a Natchez garden in 1722, and Bienville noted in 1735 that it grew well on the Mississippi River's banks. It found favor as a Louisiana crop in 1760, and became a Tennessee staple by 1796. By the turn of the century, cotton was well on its way to eclipsing tobacco and indigo as the major Mississippi river-country commodity. Sir William Dunbar, a British citizen who became one of Natchez's most successful early plantation owners after a 1763 treaty gave Great Britain all French colonial territory east of the Mississippi, wrote to one of his northern friends, "[Cotton is] by far the most profitable crop we have undertaken in this country. The climate and soil suit it exactly, and I am of the opinion that the fiber, already so fine in quality, will still be better when our lands are well cleared and the soil perfectly triturated."

But Dunbar and other European-American plantation owners were not inclined to perform these clearing and tilling tasks themselves, preferring instead to use slave labor to forge their cotton empires. After the United States acquired the Mississippi Territory from Great Britain in 1798, Dunbar wrote to a Virginia friend that slaves cost $500 cash for men and $400 for women, the price having increased since the Territory had banned slave importation from everywhere except the United States. He also noted that territorial slaves had an easier life than those in Louisiana or elsewhere in the world, supplied as they were

St. Louis Cathedral, Jackson Square, New Orleans

with good clothes, hats and shoes, heavy blankets, and all the meat, milk, vegetables, bread, melons, and potatoes they could consume. Dunbar proudly added that his slaves were afforded comfortable quarters with unrestricted use of fuel, given no nighttime work, and accorded several annual legal holidays.

Dunbar concluded by admitting that, despite the favorable conditions offered slaves by Mississippi Territory planters, "slavery can only be defended perhaps on the principle of expediency, yet where it exists, and where they so largely outnumber the whites, you must concede almost absolute power to the master." Dunbar warned, "If this principle be not admitted, the alternatives are insurrection, with all its horrors, or emancipation, with all its evils."

In his letters, Dunbar stated both the colonial case in support of slavery and the South's subsequent rationale for preserving the institution by force of arms. But history will forever record that it was the Yankee slave traders, with innocent blood on their hands, and the aristocratic French and British plantation owners, with their love of luxury and their aversion to manual labor, who originally placed the albatross of "expedient" slavery around the river-country people's necks. And although this fact in no way mitigates Southern culpability for subsequent injustices practiced upon Africans in America, it nevertheless serves as an excellent prophylactic against the spread of the seemingly incurable disease known as Northern Media Hypocrisy.

A FLOWER ON THE PEARL

Nineteenth-century Mississippi Territory frontier life was often very harsh, and all the more so when settlers couldn't lay hands on the hottest goods of the day such as pianos, fine clothes, animal hides, and honey. Fortunately for the people of the Old Natchez District, which had become a part of the Mississippi Territory in 1798, there was one man upon whom early settlers could depend to furnish them with the latest frontier merchandise. He was Louis LeFleur, a French-Canadian trader who pirogued down the Mississippi River to launch a profitable career as a traveling salesman. He began by founding a trading post on the Pearl River's banks, which later became the site of Mississippi's capital city, Jackson.

Shortly thereafter, LeFleur began bringing Natchez residents the latest items from Mobile or Pensacola by keelboat, no slight task for a man the ladies nicknamed "The Flower." Although Louis's original surname remains forever lost to history, he was such an accomplished dancer that Canada's society ladies renamed him LeFleur, for being the "Flower of the Fete" or the Dancing Flower. As vigorous on the frontier as he had been on the dance floor, LeFleur later moved his trading post to a spot on the Natchez Trace now known as French Camp. There, he made fast friends with the Choctaws, later marrying Chief Pushmataha's great-niece, Rebecca Cravat. She gave him eleven children, including a son destined to become one of the Choctaws' most famous chieftains—Greenwood LeFlore.

Colonel LeFleur later joined the American cause, fighting under loyal Choctaw chieftain Pushmataha against the British and Creeks in 1813. The last known historical notation regarding LeFleur was penned by his friend and admirer, historian J. F. H. Claiborne, who confirmed that even when LeFleur was "over 80 years old, he was an indefatigable hunter spending whole days in overflowing prairies and swamps."

But by the time of the "Flower's" passing, France's sun had long since set in the Mississippi River valley. As Claiborne noted in 1880:

> [The French] exhibited a surprising inaptitude for establishing colonies. They brought with them as much of the science and intelligence as existed in their day. They received frequent and generous supplies from [France]. . . . They had assistance from Canada and Illinois, but their administrators do not seem to have comprehended the first principles of colonization.

Instead of establishing one primary region with several nearby cities, the French spread their settlements over 1,500 miles, where communication could be had only by horse, pirogue, or canoe. They wasted their time with fruitless Indian negotiations and vainglorious explorations, and while surrounded by perhaps the "richest land in the world" were often reduced to begging sustenance from nearby Indians. They were forced to reclaim repeatedly their Louisiana capital, New Orleans, from the swamp, and although they viewed their Gulf Coast capital as little more than a "sand bank," Biloxi was the source of as "luxuriant gardens and farms as [could] be seen, where flowers, fruit, vegetables, cereals, cotton, sugar cane, and tobacco flourish under a more thrifty people."

And with France's dreams of New World domination down the drain, a new star made a swift ascent on the river country's horizon, that of a brash, young nation called the United States of America. And the Americans' jumping-off place in the Mississippi Territory was the very river that doomed De Soto and so tasked the French—the magnificent Mississippi.

Chapter Two

FATHER OF WATERS, MOTHER OF ALL ADVENTURES

No American stage enjoyed a more colorful cast of characters than did the eighteenth- and nineteenth-century lower Mississippi River valley. And at center stage was the old Mississippi Territory, with its infamous Natchez Trace. There were also its Yazoo, Tallahatchie, Sunflower, and Yocona rivers, which spawned and nurtured the wildest sort of frontiersmen imaginable, including rowdy riverboatmen, murderous land pirates, romantic steamboat gamblers, and fearless duelists. Where money was to be had, these frequently dishonest, often ruthless, and always flamboyant rogues invented new ways to grab it. And their primary route to success during this period was none other than the Mississippi River, Father of Waters and Mother of All Adventures.

Old Mississippi River Bridge, Vicksburg

DON'T HELP ME, PAL

In the mid-1700s, European treaties awarded the Louisiana Territory to Spain and all French possessions east of the Mississippi to Britain. By 1797, Spain was preparing to relinquish control of its capital at Natchez to the newly formed Mississippi Territory, which included much of present-day south Mississippi and Alabama. But before Spanish rule officially ended, itinerant preacher Barton Hannah sparked the notorious "Natchez Revolt of 1797."

At that time, Natchez's Spanish governor, Manuel Gayoso de Lemos, was very well liked by Natchez's mostly Anglo-American Protestant populace. This goodwill arose largely from Gayoso's willingness to allow Protestants to hold public religious services, despite an ordinance that required all such services to be held behind closed doors. This was apparently not good enough for Hannah, a former Virginian who strongly favored the laudable Revolutionary precept of absolute religious freedom for all.

On June 4, 1797, Hannah, buoyed by a cheering audience of his fellow Baptists (and no small amount of liquor), preached a rabble-rousing sermon against all restrictions upon Protestants enforced by the Roman Catholic-supported Spanish government. Taking offense at Hannah's attacks upon their religion, several Irish Catholics accosted Hannah and beat him senseless. After Hannah publicly threatened to take personal vengeance on the perpetrators, Gayoso had him imprisoned in the stockade. Proclaiming Hannah a martyr to religious freedom, Natchez Protestants rose up and forced Gayoso to take safety within a Spanish fort for the next two weeks.

After tempers subsided, the Spanish initiated an inquiry into the cause of the "revolt," with Hannah as its focus. After providing an interpreter to the preacher and allowing him to testify and call such witnesses as he desired, the governor called numerous Catholic witnesses who testified that Hannah had gotten drunk and obtained many names on a petition, called the "Preaching Paper," on which he had asked signers to take up arms against the Spanish government. One witness who defended Hannah was Ebenezer Dayton, a staunch Presbyterian. Dayton's explanation as to why Hannah and his supporters were innocent of the charges against them may have been partly responsible for Hannah's subsequent release and the governor's magnanimous promise not to prosecute any of the protesters.

Even so, Dayton's statement was surely not the sort of aid Hannah or anyone else of sane mind would have requested. His letter to Gayoso clearly expressed Dayton's opinion that Hannah and his fellow Baptists were "weak men of weak minds, and illiterate, and too ignorant to know how inconsistent they act and talk." Hannah was, Dayton declared, "too weak and undersigning to lay any treasonable plans."

OVER THE TOP UNDER-THE-HILL

Thanks to Bienville's establishment of Fort Rosalie in the early 1700s, Natchez became the first European-forged settlement on the Mississippi River. Much to the chagrin of the

Americans who inherited her, an early 1800s outlying region evolved alongside Natchez's aristocratic, cotton-dominated society that soon acquired a reputation as the "worst Hell hole on Earth."

Located on a narrow clay shelf bordering the Mississippi River, Natchez-Under-the-Hill stretched all the way up to the bluffs upon which the town proper rested. Under-the-Hill quickly became a haven for riverboatmen, gamblers, thieves, prostitutes, freedmen, and renegade Indians, rivaled in its excesses only by downriver New Orleans. Lined with taverns, brothels, dancehalls, and gambling dens that operated day and night, Under-the-Hill proved the quintessential den of sin. Popular British actor Tyrone Power described one of its gambling halls as "more obscene . . . than the lowest itinerant hells found at our [English] races." Said Power, "Upon the tables lay piles of silver, [and] numbers of half-dressed faded young girls lounged within the bar-room or at the doors." Hangings, shootings, knifings, and all manner of unnatural couplings proved the order of the day in the hellhole in the bluffs.

Not surprisingly, Natchez and its notorious faubourg played host to both famous and infamous frontier guests. It was there that former vice-president Aaron Burr, who had

Silver Street, Natchez-Under-the-Hill

killed Alexander Hamilton in an 1804 duel, allegedly hatched a plot to overthrow the United States government, was arrested, and was unsuccessfully tried for treason. Meriwether Lewis, who, along with William Clark, explored the Louisiana Purchase lands in 1804, later served as governor of the Louisiana Territory until he was murdered on the Natchez Trace in 1809. Jim Bowie, Andrew Jackson, and notorious robber Samuel Mason all knew Natchez well, and undoubtedly took advantage of the "entertainment" provided in Under-the-Hill. Many Natchez residents believed that God had rendered a judgment on this riverside Sodom and Gomorrah when an 1840 tornado destroyed many of the buildings and when, over subsequent years, the Mississippi River eroded the bluff against which Under-the-Hill rested.

Today, Silver Street, the sole surviving street of the original Natchez-Under-the-Hill, is part and parcel of Natchez proper, regularly visited by luxury steamboats and home to colorful bars, restaurants, shops, and, of course, a casino ship, the *Lady Luck.* However, many early-nineteenth-century visitors to the Old Natchez District met with less than good fortune, especially if they encountered the robbers, rogues, and riverboatmen inhabiting Natchez-Under-the-Hill.

ALLIGATOR MEN

In the 1820s , Kentuckians and Tennesseans floated down the Mississippi in hand-hewn vessels laden with produce and goods for sale in Natchez and New Orleans. After conducting their city business, these hardy souls walked or rode north through the river country toward their homes by way of the Natchez Trace. And while infamous land pirates ruled the Trace, rowdy riverboatmen dominated the southbound river.

Of the many available methods of transportation downriver, including the pirogue, bullboat, Mackinaw, and various styles of rafts, one of the most popular was the fifteen-foot-wide, sixty-foot-long keelboat, a craft pointed on both ends that was steered by pole and oar. Even more popular was the flatboat, a larger, flat-ended barge propelled in much the same manner as the keelboat. The capitalists operating these craft were generally known as either "flatboatmen" or "Kaintocks," and they were the toughest pioneers ever to traverse the mighty Mississip'.

Wearing little more than spike-studded brogans and linsey-woolsey trousers for their arduous treks downriver, the flatboatmen were B-A-D to the bone and not shy about mentioning it. As Mark Twain noted in his *Life on the Mississippi,* these Kaintocks often boasted of their toughness to everyone within earshot. According to Twain, typical flatboatman brag went as follows:

> Look at me, I'm the man they call Sudden Death and General Desolation! Sired by a hurricane, dam'd by an earthquake, half-brother to the cholera, nearly related to the smallpox on my mother's side! Look at me! I take nineteen alligators and a bar'l of whiskey for breakfast when I'm in robust health, and a bushel of rattlesnakes and a dead body when I'm ailing.

Other riverboatmen's boasts included "I'm *all* man, save what is lightning and wildcat and extra lightning"; "I can outswim, outsw'ar, outjump, outdrink, and keep soberer than any man at Catfish Bend"; "I'm a child of the snapping turtle"; and "I was raised with the alligators and weaned on panther's milk!" As history records, the challenge implicit in this gasconade often proved too inviting to resist.

Suffice it to say, with all these bad apples in one basket, albeit a large one like the Mississippi, trouble brewed around every bend. And while Mike Fink was generally regarded as the toughest of the Ohio River boatmen, one of the toughest regulars in port-of-call Natchez and New Orleans was Bill Sedley, a six-foot-two Kentuckian fond of saying, "If I'm agin yer, look out!"

Although he may have disagreed with this assessment, Sedley's claim to fame lay chiefly in the notorious Sedley Fight of 1822. According to witnesses, Sedley got cheated at faro by two Mexican brothers, Juan and Rafael Contreras, in a New Orleans gambling den and bordello called the Sure Enuf Hotel. Leaving in a huff, Sedley soon returned looking for trouble, yelling the familiar strain, "I'm a child of the snapping turtle." Passersby soon heard pistol shots, crashing tables, and shattering glass interspersed with repeated refrains of the "snapping turtle" brag.

Finally, when the bar doors swung open, everyone heard Sedley proclaim, "Gentlemen, walk in; it's free drinks today. The American eagle has lit on the Alleghenies." The first to enter found Sedley alive but covered with blood and gaping knife wounds. Juan Contreras lay dead under a table, and the deceased Rafael lay staked to a faro table with a knife through his midsection.

"Gentlemen," Sedley roared, "the proprietor of this here place has gone on a journey and left me in charge. Help yourself, and drink hearty."

When the law offered to fit him with a noose, Sedley took the better part of valor and headed for Kentucky. He was never seen in New Orleans or Natchez again.

QUEEN OF THE RIVERBOATMEN

Although Sedley made good his escape after the 1822 debacle, a fearless woman, the six-foot-eight, 250-pound Annie Christmas, saw fit to stick around long enough to become known as the baddest and rowdiest of the Mississippi River country toughs, according to legend. Annie was so powerful that Natchez riverboatmen, speaking of men of prodigious strength, often said that such men "were almost as strong as Annie Christmas." This mustachioed amazon once allegedly forestalled a flood by single-handedly throwing up a temporary levee, and supposedly pulled a flatboat from Natchez to New Orleans all by herself!

Annie was also an accomplished fighter, and it was widely rumored that Mike Fink himself never returned to Natchez after Annie sent him word that if he did he would be poled back up the river lashed to the keel of a boat. She wore a thirty-foot-long beaded necklace, which featured one bead for every ear or nose she'd bitten off or every eye she'd gouged out in her brawls Under-the-Hill. But not all her adventures were so mannish; she often shaved her mustache, donned women's dress, and served as a madam for a floating Mississippi River brothel.

But like most Southern belles, Annie had her softer, sensitive side. She was particularly soft on a gambler named Charlie. Whether the attraction was his good looks, fighting prowess, or the fact that his mustache was even longer and shinier than hers, Annie found Charlie impossible to resist.

Unfortunately, her new husband went gambling in New Orleans one day and came back dead. He had apparently died in a chair at the roulette table while letting his winnings ride on the red. After Charlie had won $8,000 the house refused to take any more of his bets, and when he proved unresponsive to the refusal, the croupier discovered that Annie's man had passed away in the midst of his lucky run!

The news proved to be too much for Annie's sensitive soul to bear. After spending Charlie's winnings on a lavish funeral for him, she gave their children instructions for her burial and took her own life. True to her wishes, Annie's children placed her body in a coal-black coffin on top of a coal-black barge, and floated it down the Mississippi and out to sea.

TRIAL BY RIVER

Another river brawler, Bill McCoy, achieved notoriety by virtue of a trial by river. After McCoy killed a man in a sandbar knife fight, Natchez authorities arrested him for murder. Shortly after a wealthy Natchez planter paid his $10,000 bail, McCoy disappeared upriver. On the day of the trial some weeks later, he was still nowhere to be found.

Later that evening, as the court prepared to forfeit the planter's bail money, McCoy stumbled into the courtroom, sunburned, cut almost to pieces, and exhausted to the point of near death. McCoy explained that he had left Missouri on a flatboat but, upon realizing that the boat would not reach Natchez in time for the trial, had carved a canoe out of a fallen tree and paddled several hundred miles without a breather in order to get back on time. Understandably impressed with McCoy's effort and integrity, the jury found McCoy innocent on the spot!

A PIRATE BY ANY OTHER NAME . . .

Although the keelboatmen of Natchez brought a rough and rowdy trade, they were saints compared to the infamous land pirates operating on the Natchez Trace and out of Mississippi River bank caves. In the early 1800s, the Trace was little more than a dirt road winding through an impenetrable, virgin forest of cypress, gum, willow, ash, and oak. A combination of briars, hedges, and tree trunks had created a jungle wall six feet tall on both sides of the roadway that proved the perfect, camouflaged vantage from which robbers could spring surprise attacks upon helpless passersby. The many rivers and swamps traversing the Trace made ideal hiding places for buried treasure and murder victims' bodies.

These brigands also perpetrated their crimes on the Mississippi itself, ambushing keelboats passing by their riverbank lairs just north of Natchez. But it was the opening of the Natchez Trace that gave them the opportunity to wreak unprecedented havoc upon Mississippi river-country citizens. Compared to the likes of Trace highwaymen Samuel Mason, Wiley Harpe, John Thompson Hare, and John Murrell, Western outlaws such as Jesse James, Cole Younger, and Billy the Kid were little more than schoolyard bullies with great press agents!

WITHOUT A TRACE

In 1798, the Mississippi Territory fell into American hands. A key portion of this Territory was the Natchez District, which had grown wealthy under Spanish rule. Although well serviced by the Mississippi River for southbound trade, Natchez needed a northward land route for "businessmen" to return home. An old Indian path that had existed before De Soto's arrival seemed the perfect place to begin, but for its ownership by the warlike Chickasaws.

The Choctaws had ceded their lands in the southern part of the District to the British in 1765, and had reaffirmed that cession to Spain in 1792 and again to the Americans in 1801. But the Chickasaws objected to a white-man's road through their lands on grounds that traveling whites would likely steal their horses and cattle. Of course, the whites had no

Old Sunken Trace,
near Natchez

intention of limiting their thievery to mere livestock, determined as they were to grab the Chickasaw Indians' *land.*

Accordingly, on October 24, 1801, at a place called Chickasaw Bluffs (present-day Memphis), the Americans convinced the Chickasaws to sign a treaty that allowed the federal government to clear a roadway from Natchez to Nashville. The terms of this treaty were twofold. In return for a 400-mile-long easement on their property, the Chickasaws received nine rifles, flint, shot and powder, one gun, thirty axes, thirty-six hoes, forty blankets, 100 shirts, a dozen silk handkerchiefs, two pieces of calico, fifty gallons of whiskey, 200 pounds of tobacco, and *two dozen scalping knives,* and all Trace travelers were required to obtain passes from Natchez or Nashville agents and have them countersigned by men stationed at the various taverns and stands along the Trace.

In 1815, a circuit-riding preacher described these Trace stands as "made of small poles, just tall enough for you to stand straight in, with a dirt floor . . . naked walls and no fire." In light of such accommodations, it is not surprising that a few enterprising men chose to camp out under the stars rather than abide by Trace regulations. Some of the more aggressive of these pilgrims soon wrote a terrifying new chapter in the annals of "highway robbery."

HARPEES

The most vicious highwaymen of the nineteenth century were Big (Micajah) and Little (Wiley) Harpe. Big Harpe was tall, broad shouldered, and swarthy, with lifeless eyes and dark, curly hair. Wiley had tawny, curly hair, but was not so tall and not nearly so ugly as Micajah. Dressed in fringed buckskin pants, ragged leather shirts, and wide-brimmed hats, they looked more like renegade Indians than conventional white settlers. To encounter them was to make rude acquaintance with despair and death.

The Harpes wove a trail of gruesome murders throughout Kentucky before heading for the Natchez District. They eventually moved south because their own fellows-in-crime expelled them from the worst pirate den on the Ohio River for excessive cruelty and savagery. As a joke, the Harpes had tied a hapless robbery victim to his horse and driven the animal over the cliffs. This unhappy incident proved too much even for the infamous Cave-In-Rock gang, and the Harpes headed south for friendlier hunting grounds.

But before they escaped Kentucky, Big Harpe tomahawked a sleeping fellow traveler for snoring too loudly, and then, as if to prove that his wickedness had no limits, murdered the tavern owner's wife and child. A posse pursued the brothers, and although Little Harpe escaped, the chasers put an end to Big Harpe's career. Fittingly, the aggrieved widower had the pleasure of putting a bullet in the bandit's spine. Paralyzed, but dying too slowly to suit his executioners, Big Harpe met his end by decapitation. When the widower made slow, painful work of Harpe's beheading with a dull butcher knife, the villain grew uncharacteristically eloquent, and with his last words snarled, "You're a damned rough butcher, but cut on and be damned!" Unfortunately for the Natchez District, the end of Big Harpe's criminal career in Kentucky only led to the beginning of Little Harpe's depredations in the Mississippi river country.

EXPATRIATE

Little Harpe traveled south down the Mississippi to the Natchez District, where he found an eager new partner in crime named Samuel Mason. Mason had also come south from Kentucky, but had taken a far more celebrated path than Wiley Harpe. Born in Virginia in 1750, Mason had achieved hero status as a soldier in the Revolutionary War. A well-built, handsome man, except for a "tooth which projected forwards, and could only be covered with his lip by an effort," Mason made quite a splash in backwoods Natchez, striding about with his riding crop, laying claim to fame as an upcountry planter. But Mason's good reputation ended abruptly when a witness identified him and his son as participants in a $2,300 Trace robbery of a traveler named Colonel Baker.

The Masons vehemently protested their innocence, but despite their representation by one of Natchez's best lawyers, they were ultimately convicted of horse theft. Sentences for horse thieves were cruel in those days; a first offense usually meant the branding of an *H* on one cheek and a *T* on the other, or having the culprit's ears hacked off, while a second offense usually occasioned a necktie party. But thanks to their lawyer's efforts, Mason and son got off relatively light by being merely pilloried and horsewhipped. A witness at the flogging recorded the Masons' cries of "Innocent, innocent!" as each lash ripped their flesh. After their release, the Masons stripped themselves naked, shaved their heads, and galloped out of town giving bloodcurdling Indian war whoops. Mason told terrified onlookers, "You have witnessed our punishment for a crime we never committed; some of you may see me punished again but it shall be for something worthy of punishment."

Mason was good as his word, and after linking up with Little Harpe and other desperados, he robbed and murdered a wealthy traveler, leaving a carved message on a tree near the body that read: *Done by Mason O' the Woods.* Most encounters with Mason proved tragic, but his conflict with a group of Kentucky keelboatmen had a decidedly comical tone. These Kaintocks were returning north up the Trace when, while sleeping off an evening of drunken revelry, they were surprised by Mason and his gang. Fleeing half-clothed into the woods, the Kentuckians were relieved of their weapons, goods, and river-trade earnings. One of their number, a giant of a man who had escaped with only his shirt, later led the keelboatmen, armed only with sticks and stones, through the woods to settle the score with Mason and recover their losses (and the big man's pants).

En route, their leader found his pants and, to his surprise, the four doubloons he had sewn into the waistband, which the robbers had failed to discover. Having his desire for revenge thus weakened, the giant surrendered leadership to another in the party. When the posse finally arrived at the Masons' lair, Mason's men presented their weapons and yelled,

"Clear out, or we'll kill every last one of ye!" The giant Kentuckian is said to have "outdistanced the whole party in the race back to camp."

The beginning of the end of the Mason gang's reign of terror came shortly thereafter in 1802, when territorial governor William C. C. Claiborne posted a $2,000 reward for the capture of Mason, dead or alive. In October of 1803, two men, answering to the names of James Mayes and John Setton, appeared in Natchez with Mason's head preserved in a ball of blue clay. After identifying Mason by virtue of his wolfish tooth, the two men presented their affidavits to the circuit judge and requested payment of the governor's reward. They swore they had found Mason in his camp, recognized him, gained his confidence, and cut off his head with a tomahawk while he slept. Then, just before they could collect their booty, an old Kentuckian named Captain Stump recognized their horses as those stolen from him two months earlier. "Why, that man's Wiley Harpe," exclaimed Stump.

Setton vigorously denied Stump's accusation, and the people wavered in their certainty until a Tennessean, John Bowman, said, "If he's Little Harpe, he'll have a scar under the left nipple of his breast, because I cut him there in a little difficulty we had one night in Knoxville." Closer inspection revealed a scar on Setton's body precisely where Bowman had predicted Harpe's would be. Harpe was tried for murder and hanged. After his date with the gallows, Harpe's head was cut off and mounted on a pole on the roadway that he had, in the company of men like Mason, terrorized for so many years.

A HARE-RAZING TALE

John Thompson Hare was the epitome of the romantic highwayman. He was tall, handsome, literate, religious after a bizarre fashion, often a fancy dresser, and participated in many adventures that smacked of Robin Hood lore. Once, he objected to a man's scheme of marrying young women and abandoning them after stealing their dowries. When the man challenged Hare to a fight over a young Spanish girl he was bilking, Hare beat him to a pulp. On another occasion, after Hare and his gang had relieved several victims of $13,000 in gold, Hare returned some of the gold and a watch to one of them after the fellow spun a sad tale of woe. Hare, who also occasionally played at being a gentleman, once threw an expensive party in Pensacola and invited everyone in town to attend.

In reality, Hare was more the deadly robber than the genteel, romantic adventurer. He often disguised himself as an Indian on the warpath, decorating his face with berry juice and bark stains before ambushing Trace travelers. But, as with Mason and the Harpes before him, not all of Hare's robberies came off as planned. One day he rode up to a slave trader making his way back up the Trace with a pocket full of gold. "Deliver your money," Hare said to the slaver, brandishing two pistols. "I am the Devil and I will take you to hell in a second if you don't drop that gun off your shoulder."

Initially feigning surrender, the slaver suddenly turned and fired his pistol. The black-powder discharge temporarily blinded Hare, causing his return shot to miss. As the slaver galloped off, Hare dismounted to recover his hat.

At that time, two other travelers rode up beside him. "Seen any deer hereabouts?" one of them asked.

"Yep," Hare said, mounting his horse.

"I suppose that was one you fired at just now," the other asked. "Why didn't you kill him?"

"A man will sometimes miss a thing," Hare replied. As the men rode off, Hare could only hang his head in shame as their laughter reverberated throughout the forest.

Hare's career came to an end, not on the Trace, but in Baltimore, Maryland, where he was recognized in a clothing shop by a man whose life he had once spared during a mail-coach robbery. As the always fashion conscious Hare later recalled it, "I had bought one plaid coat, lined with crimson silk at the price of $35, and one coat in the style of an officer's, at the price of $75, very dashy, when two men entered and apprehended us." Hare was hanged in Baltimore on September 10, 1818, in the presence of 1,500 witnesses, who saw vanity do to Hare what a hundred river-country posse members could not.

SIMPLY REVOLTING

The Great Western Land Pirate, as John Murrell became known, was a handsome, dark-haired dandy like Hare, often riding the best horses and usually dressed to a T. As an old judge once described him, Murrell went about "with his superfine cloth pantaloons strapped on at both extremities, his shirt fastened with tape, ribbons, and gold buttons, a superfine cloth coat on his back, a dandy silk hat with a rim three-quarters inches wide upon his head, and right and left calf-skin boots upon his feet."

Murrell was also a vicious killer like Mason and the Harpes. Once, after a lengthy walk down the Trace, he chanced upon a man on horseback. Drawing his gun, Murrell forced the man to dismount, robbed him, stole his horse, ignored his pleas for mercy, and shot him in the back of the head. "I felt sorry for him," Murrell later told a companion, "but I could not help it. *I had been obliged to travel on foot for the past four days.*" Murrell also related that he disposed of his victims by "cutting open their bellies and scraping out the guts, then filling them up with sand and throwing them into the river to feed the eels."

Well tutored in crime by his prostitute mother, a thief by age ten, and a robber and murderer at eighteen, Murrell often utilized cleverness to waylay his victims. He frequently posed as a traveling preacher in order to win their confidence long enough to rob them once he had them alone on the Natchez Trace. "I only robbed eleven men," he later bragged, "but I preached some damned fine sermons!"

But it was as a slave trader that Murrell committed many of his greatest atrocities. His favorite scheme involved offering slaves their freedom on condition that they allow him to sell them and steal them back several times on their way to freedom. After Murrell made a killing by selling and stealing the same slaves time and again, he would murder them, often women and children as well as men, disembowel them, and bury their bodies in nearby rivers or swamps.

Ultimately, he and his comrades-at-arms engineered a scheme to make themselves rich beyond all the dreams of avarice. They created an organization known as the Council of the Clan of the Mystic Confederacy, or the Mystic Brotherhood for short, whose purpose, apart from slave stealing and murdering, was to foment a great slave rebellion, which, once begun, would leave the whole of the region open to plunder by Murrell and his gang. The uprising was planned for Christmas Day 1835, but a former comrade, one Virgil A. Stewart, discovered the plan and exposed it in a book he first published in the spring of 1835. Murrell was subsequently arrested and convicted of slave stealing. Without Murrell's leadership, the insurrection was snuffed out before it began, with many of its leaders, black and white, meeting their end on the gallows. After serving his term in a Tennessee penitentiary, Murrell was released in 1844, and died a few years later of tuberculosis contracted in prison.

Old Sunken Trace, near Natchez

THE *TITANIC* OF THE MISSISSIPPI

The river country's strangest year was 1811, when a host of unusual events provoked the wonder and consternation of the populace. An excessive number of floods inundated much of the region, a "countless multitude" of squirrels inexplicably migrated south from the Ohio River valley, unprecedented sickness abounded throughout the land, a great comet lit up the sky, and a series of violent earthquakes rocked the lower Mississippi River valley, the worst causing the river itself to flow backwards towards its source! But the year's most incredible sight may have been the vision of the giant, steam-belching monster, the steamboat *New Orleans,* navigating the Ohio and Mississippi from Pittsburgh to the Crescent City at a brisk eight miles per hour. Robert Fulton's 148-foot-long invention cost $38,000 to construct and featured two masts, a stack and paddlewheels, two cabins, four berths, and comfortable furnishings for the two passengers, nine crewmen, a waiter, a cook, and the immense Newfoundland dog who shared its maiden voyage.

The *New Orleans'* celebrated eleven-day, 1,000-mile journey ushered in the glamorous steamboat era, which proved the death knell for regular traffic on the Natchez Trace. With these enormous, vapor-belching vessels plowing up and down the river, travel became faster and infinitely more pleasant than by land, although no less dangerous than before. Although a traveler's chances of drowning or being waylaid were lessened by steamboat travel, death by fire or explosion became the steamboater's daily concern.

This was especially so if the vessel's name began with an *M.* Of 723 Mississippi River steamboats built between 1811 and 1911 whose names began with an *M,* 218 met with disaster. Explosions were also common on the Mississippi's tributaries, but the Mississippi River tragedies took the greatest toll in human life. For although the ninety-four-ton *Heroine's* explosion on the Tombigbee River claimed eight lives, it paled by comparison to America's worst steamboat disaster, the *Sultana's* explosion, which occurred on the Mississippi in 1865.

On April 1 of that year, the 1,700-pound steamboat *Sultana* sprang a leak in one of her four boilers just outside of Vicksburg. Thirty-three repair hours later, she boarded 2,400 Union soldiers headed North after their release from Southern prisoner-of-war camps. With a crew of 80 and a civilian passenger count of 100, this steamboat, licensed to carry only 376 passengers, steamed for Cairo with over 2,500 people jammed on her decks. Although the crew failed to make further inspection of the leaky boiler, the *Sultana* arrived in Memphis at 7:00 P.M. on April 27. But as she headed upriver later that evening, a boiler exploded, and within twenty minutes, the entire ship was engulfed in flames. Some on board were killed by the explosion, while those trapped on the boat burned to death. Most wound up in the river.

"Men were rushing to and fro, trampling each other in their endeavor to escape," a survivor later related. "All was confusion . . . I stood for a few moments and listened to that awful wail of hundreds of human beings being burned alive in the cabins and under the fallen timbers." Another passenger found a box containing a pet alligator, bayoneted the water lizard, tossed the box into the river, stripped to his drawers, dove in the river, and pulled himself onto the box. He was soon forced to kick away other men trying to save themselves at his expense. "If they would have got hold of me," he later said, "we would have [all] drowned."

To make matters worse, it was a rainy night and the Mississippi had risen to flood stage, three miles wide. Although other steamboats came to the *Sultana*'s rescue, 1,547 lives were lost in the disaster. A postmortem revealed that the leaky boiler hadn't exploded; the culprit proved to be one of the other three "good" ones. Future precautions were taken on account of the *Sultana* disaster, and the brand of boilers utilized on that ship were never again installed in Mississippi River steamboats.

CANCEL MY REQUEST

Abe Huffstickler came to Leflore County in the 1840s when land sold for $1.25 an acre, although much of the Delta was little more than malaria-infested swampland. Bears,

Yazoo Delta Swamp

cougars, snakes, and alligators were in great abundance, and small cotton farmers faced the daunting task of clearing off jungle-like swamps under the constant threat of flood, disease, and sudden death. Huffstickler chose instead to enter the logging business, although his line of work certainly proved no easier or less risky than cotton farming. Every winter, Huffstickler hacked down hundreds of trees by hand, waited for the spring rains, then took advantage of rising flood waters by boarding his dugout canoe and floating his logs to the Yazoo River. Once on the Yazoo, he paddled himself and his logs all the way to Vicksburg, where the Yazoo met the Mississippi. After selling his timber to steamboaters and other Mississippi River businesses, Huffstickler caught the first available steamboat back up the Yazoo River.

Although the trip downriver was arduous and fraught with danger, it was no more hazardous than the steamboat ride back home, because steamboats exploded, burned. and sank on the Yazoo River with a frightful regularity. During one particularly nerve wracking steamboat trip marked by thunderstorms and raging torrents, Huffstickler found himself seated next to an increasingly agitated passenger, whom Huffstickler recognized as a well-known liar and cheat.

Unable to swim and undoubtedly suffering from a bad conscience, the man began praying aloud for heavenly deliverance through the storm. "Be silent," barked Huffstickler. "If the Lord finds out you're on board, we're sure to go under!"

TOUGHER THAN LEATHERS

Of all the steamboat captains, a former Kentuckian named Tom Leathers was the favorite in New Orleans and Natchez. From 1845 to 1879, Leathers built and captained seven steamboats, each with the name *Natchez,* and each one larger, more ornate, and faster than the last. All were decorated with hundreds of paintings of Natchez Indian chiefs and offered the latest in steamboat luxury. By the time his 1870s *Natchez* broke a speed record established by the *J. M. White* twenty-five years earlier, Leathers had acquired a reputation for putting other steamboats out of business by outracing them up and down the river. Even so, the river people considered him to be a singularly generous soul, mostly because he often gave free passage, money, and supplies to needy children, impoverished women, and sick or injured men.

But in 1870 Leathers met his match in John W. Cannon, another Kentuckian who captained the steamboat *Robert E. Lee.* Determined to prove which boat was the fastest, Leathers and Cannon left New Orleans for St. Louis on June 30, 1870, in what became known as the Great Mississippi Steamboat Race. Although Leathers took on freight and passengers, Cannon did not, and the latter further increased his speed by stripping down the *Lee* and refueling in midstream. Consequently, the *Lee* not only won the race, it established a new speed record for the New Orleans-St. Louis run of three days, eighteen hours, and thirteen minutes, which was never bested by another steamboat.

The loss of the river's most celebrated race failed to lessen Leathers' popularity. For the rest of his life he received rousing cheers and universal adulation every time he landed at Natchez. Ironically, in 1896, Leathers was killed by a hit-and-run bicyclist in New Orleans, a most unfitting end for the king of the steamboat captains.

GET A JOB

Unlike in present-day Mississippi, where legalized casino and riverboat gambling is a cottage industry in Tunica, Greenville, Vicksburg, Natchez, Philadelphia, Gulfport, and Biloxi, gambling was illegal in the old Mississippi Territory, as the following three 1817 statutes illustrate.

MISSISSIPPI GENERAL LAWS OF 1817

Act of 1801; Sect. I, § 88—Every person, whether male or female, who has no apparent means of subsistence; shall apply himself to some honest calling for his support; and if any person shall neglect to do so, or shall be found sauntering about, and endeavoring to maintain himself by gambling or other undue means, shall serve a term not exceeding ten days, at the expiration of which he shall be set at liberty, if nothing criminal appears against him. And if such a person shall be guilty of the like offence from and after the space of twenty days, he or she so offending shall be deemed a vagrant, and be subject to one month's imprisonment, and to pay all costs accruing thereon. But if such person be of noted ill fame so that he or she cannot pay the costs, such offender may receive not exceeding thirty nine lashes on his or her bare back; after which he or she shall be set at liberty.

Act of 1807; Sect. II, § 85—If any persons play at any tavern, inn, or store for the retailing of spirituous liquors, or in any other public house, or in any street, highway, or in any other open place, at any game or games, or any gaming table, or rowly powly table, or at any faro bank, or at any other gaming table, or shall bet on the sides or hand of such as do game, they shall pay fines of ten dollars, one half to the informer, and the other half to the use of the Territory. . . .

Act of 1812; Sect. I, § 105—If any person or persons shall be guilty of keeping or exhibiting any gaming table, commonly called roulette, or rowly powly, or rouge and noir [red and black], or any faro bank . . . he shall pay a fine of not less than five hundred dollars, and not more than two thousand dollars, and shall stand in the pillory three days in succession, one hour each day.

RAMBLIN' AND GAMBLIN'

The territorial and state laws prohibiting gambling never caused a moment's hesitation in those whose sole means of support was this profession. And to many 1800s gamblers on Mississippi River steamboats and in Natchez-Under-the-Hill dens, it *was* more a profession than a sport, and they devoted themselves to their trade as if it constituted their very life's blood. In games of poker, faro, blackjack, seven-up, three-card monte, and the old shell game, these bold adventurers made enormous fortunes, lost them, and recouped them, many times over. One outstanding gamesman, John Powell, lost everything by winning. In 1858, Powell won the first hand of a steamboat poker game, netting a cool $8,000. The game

Mississippi River steamboat, Natchez-Under-the-Hill

continued for three days, with Powell raking in about $50,000, most of it from a wealthy Louisiana planter. A few months later, Powell won $8,000 and luggage from a young English steamboat tourist in a two-handed poker game. The next day, the Englishman cordially greeted many of the ship's passengers, put a pistol to his head, and ended his own life. Powell sent the man's money and luggage to his family, and promptly retired from gambling. When he took it back up a year later, he did so bereft of his former luck or skill. Within another year, he was penniless, doomed to poverty for the rest of his life.

Other gamblers took their changing fortunes more philosophically. When warned that the small, Louisiana rivertown faro game he often played was fixed, the dapper Canada Bill of New Orleans replied, "I know it. But it's the only one in town!"

But the best hard-luck story may have been that of Col. Charles Starr, after lady luck had finally left him for good. When a New Orleans restaurateur, one Starr had patronized for years during the height of his gambling prosperity, demanded cash up front for the down-and-out Starr's meal, the colonel calmly exited the building. After pawning his over-coat, Starr returned and ordered the best dinner in the house. When served, he deliberately turned every dish on the table upside down and made a high-handed exit! He died of natural causes later that very evening.

The gambling houses of Natchez and New Orleans didn't always get away with shearing their victims. Once, when a steamboat passenger, a preacher no less, lost all his money in a Natchez gambling den, the ship's captain, Jack Russell, went to the house and demanded the good reverend's money back. "I'll give you until I get my boat ready to go," said Russell, "to hand over the money, and if it don't come, this house will." When the den's owner greeted Russell's terms with derision, the captain threatened to "dump this whole shebang in the river." To prove he wasn't bluffing, Russell attached a cable to the gaming house and shoved off downriver. As the gaming house began to slide into the Mississippi's murky depths, the owner quickly returned the preacher's money!

IT'S RAINING MONEY

One of the Mississippi River's greatest gamblers was New Orleans' George Devol. The son of a Revolutionary War hero, Devol had learned to cheat at cards by age eleven and by sixteen had amassed a gambling fortune of $3,000. He once cleaned out all the passengers on a steamboat and surprised his family with $400 worth of presents. Later that year, he tossed his laborer's tools into the river and said, "That's the last lick of work I'll ever do, and I will make money rain."

Although Devol was proficient at poker, faro, roulette, keno, and rouge et noir, his best game was three-card monte. This involved showing a king, queen, and jack, placing them face down, moving them around, and betting that your opponent couldn't pick a specific card. To assure himself of success, Devol—as the dealer—often employed the capper's gambit, a ruse wherein one of the cards appeared to be marked, apparently without Devol's knowledge. His opponents, upon figuring out the mark, would bet their fortunes on being able to turn up a certain card. When the marked card proved to be one they hadn't expected, Devol pocketed their money. And they couldn't accuse Devol of cheating without admitting to doing so themselves! Devol won several fortunes by resorting to this and other tricks, such as the classic stacked poker deck.

Devol was also an excellent marksman and wrestler, and he exploited these talents to great monetary success. But it was as the river's best head butter that Devol was especially revered. Head-butting, or walking off several paces, charging, and banging heads, was a popular steamboat sport, at which Devol proved to be the "head man" on the river. Unfortunately for Devol, he couldn't stay away from the shore-side faro dens, and died a poor man. "My head is old and thick," he said before shooting craps for the last time, "and maybe that's why I never had enough sense to save my money."

IN THE PINCH

In 1837, Devol taught a young black man called "Pinch" the tricks of his trade. While Devol cheated whites in monte and poker, Pinch ripped off black gamblers with a game called chuck-a-luck. This young adventurer, Pinckney Pinchback, was the freed son of a slave woman and a Mississippi plantation owner. He supported himself with river gambling for twenty-five years until he joined the Union navy at the outbreak of the Civil War. In 1862, Pinchback successfully ran a Confederate blockade on the Yazoo River at Yazoo City, leading his men all the way to New Orleans, then in Federal hands. He subsequently raised a company of black volunteers, the Corps d'Afrique, and also formed an African-American cavalry company.

Pinch went into Louisiana politics after the war, serving as state senator and lieutenant governor before becoming Louisiana's first black governor in 1872. In 1875, he signed a bill, the Mardi Gras Act, which made Mardi Gras a legal Louisiana holiday. Also during that tenure, Pinch repaid Devol for giving him his first stake on the river. After Devol had won $800 off a New Orleans police commissioner, the chief of police issued a warrant for Devol's arrest. Pinch invited Devol to the Governor's Mansion for an all-night seven-up game, and then pressured the chief into dropping all charges against his former mentor. Pinchback later graduated from a New Orleans law school in 1887, and died in Washington, D.C. in 1890.

PRESIDENTIAL SCANDAL

Although most Americans would argue that Bill Clinton's 1998 sex scandal was the worst in presidential history, they should know that the prepresidential scandal of 1791 to 1828 was actually far worse. When Andrew Jackson married Rachel Robards at Springfield Plantation, just off the Natchez Trace near modern-day Fayette, he touched off a scandal that would haunt him the rest of his political career.

As accomplished an equestrian and dancer as she was a great Carolina beauty, Rachel Donelson had married Capt. Lewis Robards, an insanely jealous man, who later accused her of committing adultery with General Jackson. Although the accusations were probably unfounded, her description of their first meeting in North Carolina suggests that the chemistry between them may have been the source of her husband's suspicions. According to Rachel's account:

> [Jackson wore] a new suit, with broad-cloth coat, ruffled shirt, his abundant suit of dark red hair combed carefully back, and, I suspect, made to lay down with bear's oil. He was six feet tall and very slender, but graceful. His eyes were handsome—a kind of steel blue. I have talked with him a great many times and never saw him avert his eyes from me for an instant.

After tiring of Robards' accusations, Jackson challenged Robards to a duel and, when the latter refused, quipped, "I've a mind to cut off your ears." Her marriage soured by Robards' unreasoning jealousy, her freedom finally assured by divorce, Rachel sailed down the Mississippi River to Natchez, meeting Jackson along the way. Their romance blossomed under the Natchez magnolias, leading to their 1791 marriage by civil ceremony at beautiful Springfield Plantation. An impressive planter-type mansion with wide upper and lower galleries supported by six Doric columns, Springfield proved the perfect place for their nuptials, more Southern than *Gone with the Wind*'s Tara and all the more romantic for having actually existed.

Unfortunately, the Jacksons' storybook marriage soon took a scandalous turn for the worse. Natchez was at the time under Spanish dominion, and marriages performed by anyone other than Catholic priests were illegal. More problematic was the fact that although Robards had indeed divorced Rachel, he had purposely failed to enroll the divorce decree properly with the Nashville circuit clerk in order to prevent her from legally remarrying.

Although they remarried in Nashville and were later celebrated in Natchez as heroes after Jackson's great 1815 victory at the Battle of New Orleans, Rachel and her husband were later accused by his political enemies of adultery and bigamy, and the scandal followed them all the way to Washington. It proved a major issue in the 1828 presidential election, won by Jackson but not before he had engaged in numerous brawls and at least one duel defending his beloved wife's honor. Tragically, the scandal contributed to the decline of Rachel's health, and she died shortly after the election and before they could take up residence in the White House.

After his wife's death, the new president, overcome with grief, cried out, "May God almighty forgive her murderers as I know she forgave them. I never can." Jackson never remarried after losing the one true love of his life. His epitaph for Rachel read, *A being so gentle and so virtuous slander might wound, but could not dishonor.*

CODE BLUE

No aspect of river-country history is more fascinating than its citizens' penchant for dueling. In the 1800s, resorting to the courts to settle disputes of honor was not considered as gentlemanly as, say, gunning down an enemy or hacking him to pieces with a sword. Such "affairs of honor" were reserved solely for gentlemen, and one of the few grounds for honorably refusing a duel was the challenger's low social standing. In this manner, many newspaper editors had their challenges go ignored, even by politicians. However, as a journalist of the time noted, as far as territorial bluebloods were concerned, "the least breach of etiquette, the least suspicion cast of unfair dealings, an aspersion against the moon, the night, the temperature," and especially any insult to Southern womanhood, would usually provoke a dueling challenge. And whereas New Orleans Creoles achieved "satisfaction" at the first drop of spilled blood under the oaks at City Park, Mississippi gentlemen often pursued the matter to incapacitation or death on Mississippi River sandbars.

Consequently, in 1807, the Mississippi territorial legislature outlawed the practice. This act referred to dueling as a "detestable" means of "adjusting or settling differences of small magnitude," arising from a "false sense of honor," and which had led to "the destruction of the lives of some valuable members of society." The law made dueling punishable by one year's incarceration and a $1,000 fine if no one was killed but called for a capital-murder charge if the vanquished party expired.

The remaining Dueling Oak, City Park, New Orleans

Although most gentlemen ignored this law, they nevertheless strictly complied with the unwritten rules of dueling, first established in Creole Louisiana as the *Code Duelo.* For example, in 1811, Mississippi territorial governor George Poindexter fought a duel with and killed one Abijah Hunt. The terms of their duel were as set out in the following letter, agreed to by the parties prior to the duel.

1. The ground shall be measured in presence of the seconds, and their principals shall then be placed at ten paces apart, facing each other.

2. The seconds in presence of each other shall charge two pistols with powder and one ball each.

3. These pistols shall be placed in the hands of the principals at their posts by their respective seconds, and shall be held with their muzzles down.

4. The giving of the word shall be decided by lot. The second who wins the privilege shall then say, slowly and distinctly—"Gentlemen, are your ready?" If both principals answer, "We are," he shall proceed thus: "One-two-three-fire!"

5. After the word "one" has been pronounced the principals may elevate their pistols, but if either shall raise it from its perpendicular position before the word "one," the second of the opposite party shall shoot him.

6. If either of the principals shall discharge the weapon before the word "fire," or shall withhold his shot after the word "fire," and then attempt to fire at this adversary, the second of the latter shall shoot him down.

7. The parties shall remain on the field until the challenging party shall declare himself satisfied, or until one of the parties shall be too much disabled to continue the fight.

8. A snap or flash of the pistol shall be considered a fire.

Despite all the precautions taken to avoid early firing, Poindexter was later and often accused of firing too soon and successfully fought many duels to defend his honor on that account.

After receiving a few years' legal reprieve, the practice was outlawed again by the Mississippi legislature in 1822, but it never fully died out until the War Between the States drained everybody's will to do mortal battle in the name of honor. Even so, the dueling spirit continued to run high in the river country long after the practice fell out of favor. In 1879, during a United States Senate battle between Southern Redeemers and South-hating Northern Radicals, Mississippi senator L. Q. C. Lamar punctuated a debate between himself and New York senator Roscoe Conklin with the language of the dueling challenge. When asked by Conklin during the floor debate if he was indeed calling Conklin a liar, Lamar responded:

> I have only to say that the Senator from New York understood me correctly. I did mean to say just precisely the words and all they imported. I beg pardon of the Senate for the unparliamentary language. It was very harsh; it was very severe; it was such as no good man would deserve, *and no brave man would bear.*

ONLY A FOOL WOULD DUEL HIM

With Mississippi law forbidding their beloved practice, Natchez and Vicksburg duelists often repaired to Mississippi River sandbars on Louisiana territory where dueling was not only legal, but as welcome as gumbo, gambling, and spoils-system politics. Of those 1820s duelists, none was more famous than Natchez's Jim Bowie. Before earning immortality at the ill-fated Alamo in 1830s Texas, Bowie made his living as a Natchez gambler and cotton land speculator. His main rival in the latter business was a Louisiana judge named R. A. Crane. In September of 1827, a difficulty arose between two of these rivals' friends that led to the most famous duel in Mississippi River history.

Bowie had already earned a reputation as a fearless duelist with knife or pistol. Over six feet tall and extraordinarily powerful and nimble, he was exceedingly cool in the face of danger or death. On one occasion, Bowie had interrupted a Natchez-Under-the-Hill card game in which a notorious card cheat, "Bloody" Bill Sturdevant, had cleaned out Bowie's good friend's son. After Bowie won the boy's money back, Sturdevant challenged him to a knife fight. After their left hands were bound together, Bowie cut his opponent's right arm with his fabled fifteen-inch, curve-tip blade, then, to his opponent's surprise, slashed the thongs that joined them, sparing Sturdevant's life. On another occasion, when passing by a Natchez plantation, Bowie had spotted an owner brutally whipping a slave. Bowie dismounted, took the man's whip, and lashed it across his back. Bowie prevailed in the duel that naturally followed, but paid his wounded antagonist's medical bill, then purchased the slave at double his value and gave the poor wretch his freedom.

But it was the brawl on the Vidalia sandbar that established Bowie as one of

Mississippi's most fearsome duelists. Although Jim Bowie didn't initiate the duel, he certainly finished it with his usual flair for the deadly dramatic. Bowie's friend, Natchez resident Samuel L. Wells, met Judge Crane's compatriot, Louisiana doctor Thomas Maddox, on a sandbar just off Natchez. However, after each man had fired two errant shots, an accord was reached between them obviating the need for further gunfire. But as they shared a bottle of wine in celebration of their newfound friendship, sparks began flying between their seconds, Bowie and Crane.

Despite the original duelists' efforts to settle the whole affair amicably, both men drew their pistols and fired. Bowie fell wounded in the leg, and when Bowie's friend, Dr. Cuney, fell mortally wounded, the others joined the melee with guns blazing and knives flashing. Another of Bowie's enemies, Maj. Norris Wright, attacked the wounded Bowie with a sword cane, but Bowie grabbed Wright's coat, pulled him downwards, and ran him through the heart with his big, curved knife. When the smoke had cleared, two men lay dead and two more nursed serious injuries.

Bowie recuperated in a Natchez bed for two months on account of his wounds and, while there, whittled a white pine model for what would later come to be known as the notorious bowie knife. The Sandbar Fight secured Bowie's reputation as a deadly opponent, a reputation that followed him all the way to Texas.

A few years later, when Bowie attended a Texas friend's sermon, and the audience hooted at the preacher unmercifully, Bowie had only to exclaim, "this man has come to preach to you, and you need preaching to; the next man that disturbs him shall fight me, and my name is Jim Bowie," to give the preacher the most respectful audience he ever encountered.

WIT: THE BETTER PART OF VALOR

To refuse a dueling challenge was considered an exceedingly cowardly act in the Old Southwest. As Monticello lawyer and orator Seargent Smith Prentiss explained to a Northern relative, if a man refuses a challenge, "his life will be rendered valueless to him both in his own eyes and those of the community." Apparently, the only way to refuse a gentleman's challenge and avoid being branded a coward was to meet the challenge with world-class wit.

A prime example concerns nineteenth-century Mississippi governor Alexander G. McNutt, who never accepted any of the numerous challenges sent him, but nevertheless earned the people's affection for having the courage to brag about his well-known cowardice. When informed that one of his enemies had issued a challenge, McNutt interrupted his own speech to tell a crowd of onlookers, "I understand that General Quitman says when he meets me he intends to whip me. Now I tell him, at this far-off distance, if he whips me it will be because he outruns me, for I have a great horror of the barbarous practice of personal violence."

HONOR HARPOONED

The dueling code decreed that the challenged man name his choice of weapons and the location for the scrap. Although a man's choice of dueling terms was often the only thing that gave him a sporting chance to survive, it occasionally saved him from participating in the duel at all. Harvey, Louisiana, located on the Mississippi River across from New Orleans, is named for the skipper of a whaling ship who came to the river country in the 1840s. After Harvey and one Albert Favre came to blows during a New Orleans Creole's party, Favre challenged Harvey to a duel. What Harvey lacked in dueling skills he more than made up for in good sense, choosing terms of "ten-foot-long whaling harpoons at twenty paces." Favre wisely decided that he hadn't really been insulted by the skipper, and the proposed duel never took place.

SLEDGEHAMMERS AT DAWN

One of New Orleans' most accomplished duelists was wealthy Creole statesman Bernard de Marigny. In 1817, the hot-tempered Marigny challenged an American blacksmith, James Humble, to an *affaire d'honneur* over a joke Humble had told at Marigny's expense. Although Humble realized he had no chance to survive a duel with such an able marksman and deft swordsman, he made the most of his two advantages, his sense of humor and the fact that, at seven feet tall, he towered over the five-foot-nine Creole. Humble declared his terms of combat as ten-pound sledgehammers in six feet of water in Lake Pontchartrain! Realizing that he was "in over his head," Marigny laughed and hugged his old friend, and bloodshed was averted.

TILL DEATH DO US PART—NOT!

One tragic story associated with dueling concerns Helen Johnstone and Henry Vick, whose love affair was ended by a fatal 1859 duel. Helen was the daughter of John Johnstone, the owner of Annandale, a plantation located several miles north of Jackson, in present-day Madison. The son of Vicksburg's founder Newit Vick, Henry was a dashing young romantic who had fallen deeply in love with Helen.

Shortly before their wedding day, Henry fought a duel in New Orleans, much to Helen's chagrin. Her concerns proved justified when Henry was killed because he held his fire, having given Helen his word that he would never take another man's life. When his body arrived at Annandale on their wedding day, the distraught Helen insisted that the wedding take place as planned, going so far as to place his ring upon her finger during the ceremony. She became known as the Bride of Annandale, and her ghost is often seen brooding on a bench at the lovely Chapel of the Cross, the antebellum Episcopal church where the pacifist dueler Henry Vick was laid to rest.

Chapter Three

PROFESSIONAL DISCOURTESY

Following the demise of river-trade violence, wholesale lawlessness in the towns, and unimpeded highway robbery on the Trace, a different breed of professional men and women set up shop in the Mississippi river country. Itinerant preachers, traveling salesmen, dime-store lawyers, two-bit actors, enterprising prostitutes, quack doctors, and crafty politicians did their part to make frontier life as interesting as possible. And although many dedicated professionals such as John Sharp Williams and William Johnson gave their blood, sweat, and tears to help mold the river country into the American paradise it later became, there once was a time when a few white-collar mountebanks prompted the wiser among the populace to tighten their grips on their purse strings, believe less of what they heard, and laugh at much of what they saw!

Lafitte's Blacksmith Shop, New Orleans

TRICKIN' IN THE NAME OF THE LORD

Not all the nineteenth-century Mississippi river-country con artists were gamblers, politicians, or hucksters. Some were preachers, although not all of them were of the mainstream religious variety. One of the worst was New Orleans' John Montaigne, also known to his fellow 1840s voodoo practitioners as "Doctor John." A large, coal-black man with a tattooed, scarred face and fierce, blazing eyes, Montaigne claimed to read minds, cure ills, predict the future, and cast gris-gris spells. He certainly dabbled in the occult and treated his illiterate, impoverished clients to more extortion, bribery, betrayal, and roguery than they had ever suffered at the hands of "decent" society. He also spied on wealthy Creole socialites, blackmailing those who wished to keep their sexual indiscretions under wraps. Eventually, though, Doctor John reaped what he had sown. After paying a tutor to teach him to write, he signed his name to a blank check during an ostentatious show of wealth, only to discover later that his rash act had cost him his entire fortune!

Upriver in the Natchez District, a host of courageous, dedicated preachers, including early-1800s Methodist circuit rider and Vicksburg's founder, Newit Vick, brought the gospel to the frontier. But like many of New Orleans' celebrated voodoo doctors and queens, some of the Territory's itinerant preachers were scoundrels of the lowest sort. The most renowned was Methodist circuit rider Lorenzo ("Crazy") Dow, who came downriver to Natchez in 1804. A Connecticut Yankee in King Cotton's domain, the long-haired, shaggy-bearded Dow cut quite a figure in his black frock coat, but it was his wild-eyed expression than earned him his sobriquet.

Preaching in log churches, cotton fields, and Natchez-Under-the-Hill drinking halls, Dow raised Cain wherever he could attract a paying audience. "Sinners," he was often heard to exclaim, "you are making a beeline from time to eternity!" But although his favorite weapon against Satan was his thunderous oratory, Dow was not above enlisting trickery to stir his listeners to repentance and generosity.

Once, before preaching on the subject of Judgment Day, Dow placed a little black boy with a trumpet in the top of a tall pine tree. Then, when he reached the part of his sermon that referred to Gabriel trumpeting Armageddon, he signaled the boy to cut loose on his horn. Panic ruled the day until the ruse was discovered. Faced with an angry mob, Dow reversed his fortune by inquiring, "Brethren, if a little Negro boy blowing on a tin horn can fright you so, how will you feel when the Last Day really comes?"

FIRST, LET'S KILL ALL THE CRITICS

It's been said that where there's culture, there's theater, and amateur theater came to the Mississippi river country on February 4, 1806, in the Natchez City Tavern's production of *The Provoked Husband*. In 1814, Shakespeare reached the Natchez stage in a production of *Othello*. Within three years, professional companies were treading the boards in Natchez, and by the 1830s, theater was alive and well in Vicksburg and Jackson. Many famous actors of the day appeared on river-country stages, including Junius Brutus Booth, Edwin Forrest, George Holland, and Louisa Lane, the grandmother of John, Lionel, and Ethel Barrymore.

The Natchez theater, originally a hospital built in grand Spanish style in the midst of a graveyard, proved to be the perfect meeting ground for that wealthy city's aristocrats. Describing the Natchez theater's affluent patrons in the twentieth century, Irishman Tyrone Power said, "They were the planters of the neighboring country, many of whom came nightly to visit the theater. . . . A finer set of men I have rarely looked upon." He deescribed them as "picturesque" in their white or green tunics, wide-brimmed fur-covered Spanish hats, leather leggings, and cavalry boots.

But almost every silver cloud has a black lining, and the theater's cross to bear has always been the presence of those savage, heartless beasts—the critics. Whether claiming to be Natchez's moral watchdogs or cruelly criticizing others who did what they themselves could never do, 1800s Natchez theater critics feasted upon local thespians' supposed foibles. The first Natchez review came in the *Mississippi Republican* in 1818, when one "Dramaticus," unwilling to admit his real name, panned a performance of *Catherine and Petruchio.* From that moment, the Natchez theater was never safe from such shameless vituperation.

Regarding an 1818 performance of *The Wonder! A Woman Keeps* a Secret, critic "XYZ" wrote, "With mingled feelings of contempt and indignation . . . we witnessed the performance of [the playwright's] indecent comedy. [The theater's managers] have entirely mistaken the taste of our citizens if they suppose that coarse and vulgar allusions, and indecent expressions, are calculated for this meridian."

The playwright might have responded that at least she had the courage to put her name on her work, and had substantially more creative talent than anyone identifying himself by the pedestrian nom de plume "XYZ."

Castigating a director's nontraditional casting of an 1839 performance of *Romeo and Juliet,* another wag moaned:

> We are sorry to say that she [Miss Ellen Tree] was not, could not be, the lover Romeo. . . . She is a lady, and an accomplished one. Romeo was a man; how can a woman know those masculine traits?

This raises the obvious question—what qualifies a critic to critique, apart from a sassy tongue and doltish perspective?

One of the few actors these early critics universally adored was Junius Booth, cousin to Abraham Lincoln's assassin. Of Booth's 1839 star turn in *King Lear,* one critic wrote in the Natchez *Free Trader,* "It is said by the gossips that Booth has a manic stripe in the texture of his brain that makes him one of the most illustrious of kingly madmen."

One might counter that it would have been preferable for the texture of that critic's brain, and not that of Mr. Lincoln's, to have been splattered across Ford's Theater by Junius Booth's cousin, the truly maniacal John Wilkes Booth.

EVERYONE'S A JURIST

As with the greatest of their lawyerly kind—Cicero, William Blackstone, and Oliver Wendell Holmes—so it was when the bench and bar first came to the Old Southwest's Mississippi Territory; lawyers and judges have never seen eye to eye. As historian Joseph Baldwin relates, two early 1800s examples suggest that their contests of verbal volleyball often led to metaphorically blackened eyes.

A territorial attorney, much disposed toward drinking, once moved to dismiss his own case, but did so in the vernacular of the times, which referred to an appropriately sinking ship:

Judge. What is your pleasure, counselor?

Lawyer. If it please the court, I will "take water."

Judge. Well, if you do, you will astonish your stomach most mightily.

Another judge, growing impatient at a lawyer's insistence upon pursuing a matter after the judge had rendered his ruling, decided to put the lawyer in his place:

Judge. You have been practicing, sir, before this Court long enough to know that when this Court has once decided a question, the propriety of its decision can only be reviewed in the High Court of Errors and Appeals! Take your seat, sir!

Lawyer. If your honor please, far be it for me to impugn in the slightest degree the wisdom and propriety of your honor's decision! I merely designed to read a few lines from the volume I hold in my hand, that your honor might perceive how profoundly ignorant Sir William Blackstone was upon this subject.

Or in the courtroom vernacular, "Objection sustained," with a further order of humble pie on the side.

LAWYER IN THE DEVIL'S DEN

Insurance companies, doctors, and large corporations are among those who often accuse lawyers of being modern-day pirates who plunder the wealth of others. However, in 1813, the river country experienced a one-on-one battle between a lawyer and a real pirate that left no doubt as to which profession produced the most merciless and adept plunderers. In that year, prominent New Orleans attorney John R. Grymes undertook to represent the brother of the bayou's notorious buccaneer, Jean Lafitte.

The tall, handsome, sturdily built, raven-haired, mustachioed Lafitte, who usually dressed in a green uniform and otter-skin cap, had already grown rich smuggling slaves into New Orleans and selling them out of his Royal Street blacksmith store when Louisiana governor William C. C. Claiborne offered a $500 reward for his capture. Exceptionally popular with Louisianans for his civilized manners and pleasant disposition, Lafitte scoffed at the governor's proclamation and posted bills throughout the French Quarter offering a $1,500 reward for the governor's capture. But shortly after Claiborne indicted the whole Lafitte gang, Jean's brother, Pierre, fell into the governor's hands.

Lafitte promptly hired both Grymes, a district attorney who resigned his office to take the case, and Edward Livingston, the son of the judge who gave George Washington the presidential oath, to spring Pierre from jail. After they failed to accomplish the task, Lafitte broke Pierre out of jail and spirited him back to their lair on Grand Terre Island in Barataria Bay. When the attorneys asked if he still planned to pay their fees of $20,000 each, Lafitte sent them word that he would do so, on condition that they came to Grand Terre to get it. Livingston wisely declined, but Grymes accepted Lafitte's terms and assured Livingston that he would also recover his colleague's fee, for a 10 percent commission, of course. Once on Lafitte's territory, Grymes gambled away both his $20,000 and his 10% commission (comparable to several hundred thousand of today's dollars), but returned to New Orleans with Livingston's fee.

Grymes might have become the river country's first butt of endless lawyer jokes had he not been a more accomplished duelist than he was a criminal defense lawyer or gambler!

HI HO, HI HO, TO STORYVILLE WE GO

During the early 1800s, prostitution was a major form of entertainment for many Mississippi river-country pioneers, especially at Natchez-Under-the-Hill, where houses of ill repute and "floating bordello" steamboats were as common as dirt and muddy water. But by the 1890's, the profession had been officially outlawed in most Mississippi towns, and Natchez's working girls had been forced to seek employment in New Orleans, the queen city of Southern prostitution. In 1898, Crescent City fathers passed an act that established Storyville, a thirty-eight-block area including parts of Bienville, Conti, and St. Louis streets, as the lawful home for two-dollar-, three-dollar-, and five-dollar-a-throw brothels and assignation houses.

And since few commercial enterprises flourish in these United States without resorting to clever advertisement, Storyville soon witnessed the birth of several red-light-district publications, including the last and most famous—the *Blue Book*—which first appeared in 1895. According to historian Herbert Asbury, excerpts from these advertisements included glowing tributes to the various madams and their girls:

—Martha Clark, 227 N. Basin: Her women are known for their cleverness and beauty. Also, in being able to entertain the most fastidious of mankind.

—The Club, 327 N. Franklin: Come and join the club and meet the members.

—Diana and Norma, 213 N. Basin: Their names have become known on both continents, because everything goes as it will, and those that cannot be satisfied there must surely be of a queer nature.

—Edna Hamilton, 1304 Conti: As for women, she has an unexcelled array, who, aside from their beauty, are all of high class and culture.

—The Studio, 331 N. Basin: Everything goes here. Pleasure is the watchword.

—Grace Lloyd, 338 N. Franklin: A visit will teach you more than the pen can describe.

—Mary Smith, 1538 Iberville: A pleasant time for the boys.

—Countess Willie V. Piazza, 317 N. Basin: If you have the blues, the Countess and her girls can cure them.

While many paying customers undoubtedly found a cure for the blues in the Storyville district, others probably came for the jazz, which had its origins in Storyville whorehouses. In 1895, a seven-member band of twelve- to fifteen-year-old boys calling themselves the Spasm Band began playing in brothel saloons. With a gas pipe for a singer's megaphone, a fiddle fashioned from a cigar box, a harmonica, a cowbell, a kettle, whistles, horns, and a gourd filled with pebbles, these boys gave a bold new music form to the world. They later changed their band's name to the Razzy Dazzy Spasm Band, and when an experienced adult band "borrowed" both their name and their repertoire, the boys protested sufficiently to force the new band to change its name to the Razzy Dazzy Jazzy Band. And the rest, as they say, is river-country musical history!

QUACK, QUACK, SWAMP FEVER'S BACK

Swamp fever, as malaria was once known in the Mississippi Delta, played havoc with 1800s pioneers, especially those establishing communities on the Yazoo River's banks. During the "sickly season" from June to October, one-third of the Delta's population succumbed to the chills, fever, headaches, and thirst occasioned by the disease. Because women were particularly susceptible to swamp fever, it became fashionable for Delta suitors to propose marriage by asking the honor of buying their true love's *coffin.* Malaria was still going strong as late as the year 1920, when swamp fever claimed 477 lives in seventeen Delta counties.

And although a Mississippi doctor—Henry Perrine—first prescribed quinine for the dreaded mosquito-induced plague, there were no small number of quacks offering half-baked "remedies" with no curative effect upon the patient, but which significantly increased these sawbones' bank accounts. One patent medical firm issued an 1898 report stating, "It is generally understood that malaria poisons are absorbed into the systems from the atmosphere. . . . It is absolutely impossible to prevent malarial germs from entering the system, but it is altogether possible to prevent their doing harm after they get in."

Some of the cures frequently proposed for malaria came in the form of a tonic or a pill, with names like Grove's Chill Tonic 666, Smith's Bile Bean, Liquozone, and Rich's Tasteless Chill Tonic. These tonics were not only advertised as cures for malaria; they also claimed to provide relief for asthma, ulcers, headache, weakness, lameness, mental strain, upset stomach, common cold, gallstones, tuberculosis, cancer, acne and bad breath. One manufacturer made a memorable guarantee to outdo the competition with an advertisement that read, "If you are taking the large old-fashioned griping pills, try Carter's Little Liver Pills, and take some comfort. A man can't stand everything."

While none of these cure-alls offered the least therapeutic effect, some of the tonics may have helped patients to forget their woes; many were over 100-proof alcohol! And although it was traveling salesmen, not doctors, who usually prescribed such measures, some doctors withheld the real cure until after their malaria-stricken patient's third or fourth visit on grounds that four fees were better than one. However, it should be noted that with tonic salesmen in the 1800s, as today with chiropractors and naturopaths, doctors rose to the occasion of combating the evils of potential quackery and certain competition. The American Medical Association issued a report that one of these alleged malaria cures, Liquozone, was made of nine-tenths of 1 percent sulfuric acid, three-tenths of 1 percent sulfurous acid, and the rest plain water!

SHAVE AND A HAIRCUT: TWO BITS AND A BOTTLE OF BEAR OIL

Known in the 1830s as the "Free Negro of Natchez," William Johnson was one of around 520 free Mississippi blacks, and he acquired a small fortune as a barber, landlord, moneylender, slave owner, and small farmer. He also left a diary, from which we may derive a fairly accurate picture of antebellum Natchez's cost of "doing business." Johnson recorded that expenses incurred during an 1831 business/pleasure trip from Natchez to New Orleans included an $8 steamboat fare to the Crescent City and a $10 return-trip tab, plus $63 for barbershop perfumery, $30 for a violin, 75 cents for a barrel of flour, 12 cents for two steaks, $12 for a carriage ride for two, $3 for lunch for two, and 50 cents for "Sensual Pleasures." A month in New Orleans cost Johnson a total of $136, while a week's worth of clothes washing ran him a mere $4.

Regarding more serious business, Johnson wrote that, in 1835, barbershop costs were

Razorstrap 75

2 scissors 1.50

8 razors 5.37

[which the enterprising capitalist resold at a rate of 2 for $5.00]

3 cakes of soap 1.25

1 powder & puff 1.25

2 bottles lavender wate 17

Oh yes, and the cost of an 1830s shave and haircut was actually two bits (.25), but the accompanying bottle of Bear Oil and one cake of soap cost an additional six bits (.75)!

THEY'S POLITICIANS IN THEM THAR WOODS

According to legend, the Mississippi Delta, which includes Greenville, Indianola, Greenwood, Cleveland, Clarksdale, Tunica, and many other cotton-dominated river towns, "begins in the lobby of the Peabody [the famous Memphis hotel] and ends at Catfish Row in Vicksburg." This region, where cotton is king and the river is queen, is famous for producing more than muddy water, antebellum mansions, the blues, and an ideal alternative to polyester apparel. It is also renowned for producing more than its share of flamboyant politicians. One planter-statesman who followed in the proud tradition of L. Q. C. Lamar and Edward C. Walthall was Yazoo County's John Sharp Williams, who served Mississippi as both governor and U.S. senator in the late 1800s and early 1900s.

Famous for both his razor-sharp wit and his propensity to imbibe, Williams once called upon Sen. LeRoy Percy in Prohibition-era Greenville and beseeched his colleague to obtain some whisky. When Percy returned an hour later complaining about paying twenty-five dollars for a bottle, Sharp said, "Ah, at last we've found a place where they appreciate the true value of liquor."

During a debate in the U.S. Senate, one of Sharp's opponents attempted to make sport of the old senator on account of his drinking. "Well," said the Yankee congressman "whatever else may be said of me, when I come into the Senate chamber, I always come with full possession of my faculties."

"What difference does that make?" asked Williams, to the amusement of his colleagues.

A strong opponent of Theodore Roosevelt's economic policies, the irreverent Williams once penned his own version of the Apostles' Creed in response to Roosevelt's post-African safari announcement that he intended to seek a third presidential term as the Bull Moose candidate.

ROOSEVELT'S CREED

I believe in Theodore Roosevelt, maker of noise and strife, and in Ambition, his only Creed. He was born of the love of power and suffered under Taft; was crucified, dead and buried. He descended into Africa. The third year he rose from the jungle and ascended into favor, and sitteth on the right hand of his party, whence he shall come to scourge the licked and the dead. I believe in the Holy Outlook, the Big Stick, the forgiveness of political activities, and the resurrection of Presidential Ambitions, and the Third Term Everlasting.

Ever the forward-thinking individual, Williams gazed into Mississippi's future and saw the evils lurking there, including the Populist movement championed by James K. Vardaman and Theodore Bilbo and the coming welfare state. He resigned from politics in 1923, saying, "I would rather be a hound dog and bay at the moon from my Mississippi plantation than remain in the U.S. Senate." In a letter to a Virginia Law School student later that year, the retired Williams issued the following tirade from his beloved Cedar Grove Plantation:

You ask for what "principles" the Populist party stood? None. It stood for discontents. It was a blind man reaching out to catch cures for economic diseases. Cotton and wheat were both being sold for less than the cost of production. The habit had grown up of looking to "the Government" for "relief." . . . It proceeded so far as to become a revolt against superiority of intellect, of education, of birth. . . . Men such as Vardaman in Miss., and their ilk elsewhere became later the interested spokesmen of discontent, distress, and envy. . . . You know it is easy always to persuade an audience that they are "bad off," because there is never a time when people do not think they might be better off and that they ought to be. There is never a time when there are not inequalities and even positive injustices, nor will people learn that these have to be cured from within and not from without—by love and service done and received and not by Acts of Congress.

Within a scant few years, and for the balance of the twntieth century, many good river-country citizens would be saying, "Amen to that, brother Williams!"

Chapter Four

DRUMS ALONG THE MISSISSIPPI

The American Indian had been comfortably ensconced in the lower Mississippi River valley for thousands of years before De Soto crossed the Tombigbee River in 1541. In the sixteenth century, 8,000 Chickasaws occupied Mississippi's northeast hill region, over 20,000 Choctaws resided in the fertile lands to the south, and around 6,000 sun-worshiping Natchez inhabited a portion of the eastern bank of the Mississippi near present-day Natchez. Of the smaller nations, the Yazoo, Tunica, Houma, Chakchiuma, and Koroa were the principal tribes in the Yazoo River valley, while the Pascagoula, Biloxi, and Acolapissa constituted the major coastal tribes. Whether these tribes suffered extinction, as did the Natchez, left on the Trail of Tears with the Chickasaws, or remained in their ancestral homelands as did the Choctaws, their stories are as compelling as those better-known tales told around Western plains campfires or on the Hudson River's celebrated banks.

Choctaw Indian Festival at Ridgeland on Natchez Trace Parkway

ATALA'S SONG

The Natchez produced their own version of *Romeo and Juliet,* and as with Shakespeare's version, theirs was also grounded in fact. As their story goes, Chactas, a Natchez warrior, had been taken captive by the Muskogee. Before they could put him to torture, a Muskogee maiden, Atala, fell in love with the captive brave. She helped him to escape, and during their journey to Chactas's Natchez lands they fell deeply in love.

Unfortunately for the star-crossed lovers, Atala's mother had been converted to Christianity by the French and had passed her beliefs on to her daughter. Torn between her previously made vow to give herself completely over to the "virgin queen" and her unquenchable desire for Chactas, Atala fell ill with anxiety. When they encountered a priest named Father Aubry, the cleric was so impressed with the depths of their feelings for each other that he told them that true Christianity could never come between two so deeply in love.

Although Aubry offered to relieve Atala from her vow, his generous offer came too late; Atala died the next day. After burying his true love, the brokenhearted Chactas returned to his Natchez tribe. Atala's song, which was sung by the Natchez for generations, goes in part, "Happy are those that never beheld the smoke of strangers' feasts and only sat down at their father's banquets."

WHITE APPLES CAN BE BITTER

One of the most bittersweet North American love stories occurred in 1729. A Natchez princess, Stellona, fell in love with a handsome French lieutenant, Chevalier de Mace. The Natchez already resented the occasional romances between their maidens and the dashing French soldiers, but when the French proved unwilling to settle for a liberal share of the Natchez's crops and demanded full ownership of ancestral farmlands, the Natchez invited the Choctaws and Chickasaws to a council of war. The council decided to launch a joint assault against the French garrison at Fort Rosalie in twenty days. To assure a well-coordinated attack by distant war parties, and in lieu of a jointly held calendar, each tribe set a quiver of twenty arrows in its temple and broke one arrow a day, with the three tribes agreeing to attack from separate locations on the day of the last arrow's breaking.

Stellona discovered the plot and informed her lover, Sieur de Mace, who in turn advised his commandant, who foolishly imprisoned Mace for spreading false rumors of war. Unable to convince her father, the Great Sun of White Apple Village, to call off the attack, Stellona snuck into the Natchez's temple and broke two of their arrows. Consequently, the Natchez attacked the French two days early without the other two tribes' aid.

Although the New Orleans Jesuit, Father Le Petit, later claimed that the Natchez attacked early to seize two richly laden barges that arrived at the fort on September 26, regardless of what prompted the attack, the Natchez succeeded in wiping out Fort Rosalie, and slaughtering 35 women, 56 children, and 138 Frenchmen, including Sieur de Mace. But because they kept all the prisoners and booty for themselves, the Natchez incurred their confederates' resentment and made permanent enemies of the Choctaws. Consequently, when the French launched a counterattack, the Choctaws joined them, and together they completely annihilated the Natchez. Stellona's new Indian lover was killed in the battle of White Apple Village, and the miserable maiden was taken prisoner by the French.

HELL'S KITCHEN

The Natchez were similar to the French intruders in many respects. Like France, their nation also had an aristocratic, highly privileged upper class—the Suns—who referred to the lower classes as "stinkards." The Natchez were led by a king who attained his throne by heredity and who presided over a national religion. And although the Natchez buried their dead in large, earthen burial mounds, as opposed to European-style cemeteries, they, like the French, also had their own peculiar version of eternal heaven and hell. According to Father Le Petit, who first encountered them in 1700, the Natchez believed that in the afterlife, the good were treated to a perpetual feast of green corn, venison, and melons, while the bad were fated to endure an eternal diet of alligator and spoiled fish!

INDIANS—3, FROGS—1

After the White Apple Village massacre, the Natchez ceased to exist as a nation. A few survivors moved to Louisiana, while others traveled north to join their allies, the Chickasaws, whose nation lay between the Tombigbee and Tallahatchie rivers. Tall, well built, and of unequaled courage and intrepidity, the Chickasaws never suffered defeat at Spanish or French hands. But after the Chickasaws granted asylum to the homeless Natchez and refused French demands to hand them over, the sons of France decided to try their luck against the Chickasaws one more time. French hopes rested upon the shoulders of Iberville's brother, the French colonial governor, Jean Baptiste Le Moyne, Sieur de Bienville. This proved a poor choice, for, although Bienville succeeded in founding settlements at Biloxi, Natchez, and Baton Rouge and would later be regarded as the father of New Orleans, in the northeast Mississippi river country, he was destined to became the Chickasaws' favorite whipping boy.

In 1736, Bienville planned and led a pincher assault upon the Chickasaws, their Shawnee allies, and the surviving Natchez. According to his plan, Bienville's first officer, Pierre d'Artaguette, would attack from the north, and Bienville would move against the natives from the south. The Chickasaw villages were located near present-day Tupelo, with Ackia defended by the peace chief, Imayatabe le Borgne, who did not desire the conflict, and Ougoula Tchetoka defended by the war chief, Mingo Ouma, who wished to protect the Natchez at the expense of war.

D'Artaguette and his Choctaw allies attacked Ouma's village on May 20, 1736. Although the Frenchman had preferred to wait for reinforcements, the Choctaws had insisted on striking at first light. This proved to be a poor decision, as the Chickasaws routed the French and burned twenty of their number at the stake, including d'Artaguette and Fr. Antoine Senat.

That same day, unaware of the circumstances to the north, Bienville and his Choctaw allies made camp outside Ackia, the peace chief's village. Although the Chickasaw peace chief, Imayatabe, sent the French a calumet of peace, Choctaw chief Red Shoe, who sought to prevent any accord between the French and his rivals, the Chickasaws, ordered his braves to fire on the peace party without Bienville's permission. In the ensuing brush fight, the Choctaws sustained heavy losses and opted out of any further fighting. All-out war being thereafter unavoidable, the French then attacked the Chickasaws' earthworks. They, too, were routed, and Bienville and his entire company would have suffered total annihilation had not their Choctaw allies covered their retreat.

Bienville later blamed his defeat on the cowardice of his French troops. "I was still less able to foresee the cowardice of the troops that I had under my orders," he said in a June 28, 1736, letter to French Marine Minister Maurepas. "It is true that when one considers the wretched blackguards that are sent here as recruits one ought never to flatter oneself that one will make soldiers of them. The unfortunate thing is to compromise the honor of the nation and *to expose officers to the necessity of getting themselves killed."*

While few would list making war among the things the French do well, it would be closer to the truth to say that the Choctaws, with their fervent desire to foment hostilities between the French and Chickasaws, ultimately caused Bienville's undoing. There's an old saying, "When in France, do as the French." Bienville may have benefited from an ancient Mississippi river-country axiom—"When dealing with native guerilla fighters in the woods, you should pack a good lunch if you're pinning your hopes on French soldiers in brightly colored uniforms who'd rather make love than war!"

CHICKASAW HEAVEN

British religious leaders John and Charles Wesley introduced Methodism to the world in 1738. Two years earlier, on July 20, 1736, and two months after the Chickasaws had routed Bienville at Ackia, John Wesley interviewed Chickasaw chief Paustoobee regarding the latter's religious beliefs. When informed that the Indians believed in their own version of the Trinity headed by the One who lives in the Clear Sky, Wesley asked whether they also believed that the One had made their beloved Sun and Clouds. "We cannot tell," the chief sagely replied. "Who has seen?" Although the chief said he was fairly certain that the One had fashioned man "out of the ground," when asked if the One loved him, he again replied, "I don't know. I cannot see Him."

Paustoobee informed Wesley that he and his people often spoke of the One, both in peace and in war, whenever they met together. When asked about the afterlife, the chief opined that the souls of "Red Men" wandered the earth near the place where they died but offered no opinion as to the repository for "White Men's" souls, saying simply, "We can't tell. We have not seen." When Wesley inquired as to whether the Chickasaws were interested in knowing about the white man's religion, Paustoobee answered, "We have no time now but to fight. If we should ever be at peace, we should be glad to know."

The chief allowed that, although the One could save the Chickasaws from their enemies, he was uncertain whether He would do so. "We have so many enemies around us," Paustoobee said, "that I think nothing but death. And if I am to die, I will die like a man. But if He will have me to live, I will live." Finally, when asked if his tribe would ever wish to know everything the white men knew, Paustoobee replied that his people "believe the time will come when the Red and the White Men will be one."

NO FAULT, NO PROBLEM

One of the Chickasaws' most charming customs was their marriage ritual, in which a brave, by way of marriage proposal, sent his prospective bride enough calico to fashion herself a dress. He sent the material bound up in a shawl or handkerchief, with an attached note asking the maiden's parents' approval of the proposed betrothal. If they agreed, they handed the girl the package. If she accepted it, the marriage was on. The man then dressed in his formal buckskin attire, painted his face with vermilion, and called on his bride-to-be. After making small talk, the young man and his intended father-in-law took supper by themselves. The marital bed was then prepared for the couple, who promptly consummated the marriage.

Just as charming but substantially less complicated was the Chickasaw no-fault divorce arrangement. Upon growing dissatisfied with the marital relationship, either mate could simply strike out on his or her own. This procedure was likely abetted by Chickasaw inheritance laws, which provided that a deceased person's goods passed only to his or her siblings. This Chickasaw divorce ritual constituted the first instance of no-fault divorce in the Mississippi river country. However, no-fault divorce was not adopted by whites until 1990, European Americans being as inferior to Native Americans in common sense as they were in swamp battle tactics.

LUCK OF THE SCOTTISH

Although the Chickasaws won all their major battles with the French and Spanish, they lost a few minor skirmishes with the British and Americans, as illustrated by this late-1700s tale of a Scottish frontiersman's narrow escape from a Chickasaw brave's scalping attempt. Sporting the day's customary wig with a long queue hanging down the back of his neck, a Scotsman had slipped away from Natchez's Fort Panmure to steal some sweet, green Indian corn. Discovered and chased by a brave, the Scotsman had almost reached the fort when the Natchez overtook him. The brave grabbed him by the hair and attempted to scalp him, but received a big surprise when the white man's scalp came off easily and bloodlessly. As the Indian stood there gaping at the wig, the Scotsman made good his escape!

STARCH IN THEIR PETTICOATS

The menfolk weren't the only hardy souls on the frontier. Many Indian women went into battle alongside their husbands, and some of the white frontierswomen acquitted themselves quite honorably in troubled times, including one femme fatale who held her own under extreme Chickasaw duress. In the late 1790s, Indian attacks on frontier forts were still a relatively common event, so when Natchez-area fighting men absented themselves from forts on errands or other pressing business, they left the old men behind to protect the women from surprise attack.

Historian J. F. H. Claiborne relates that on one such occasion, a man named Clayton, several women, and another elderly gentleman holed up in the blockhouse of a fort to defend themselves from a furious Chickasaw raid. The other old man lost his nerve and began telling the women their deaths were imminent and they should resort to their final prayers. One woman, steeled with the frontier fighting spirit, told the old coot that if he went on about "praying" any further she would "blow his brains out!" With young boys reloading their rifles, Clayton and the women fired away with such favorable effect that the Indians took to flight, believing the fort to be defended by regular soldiers.

PUSHMATA ENVELOPE

Of the Choctaws, both their friends and enemies agreed that they were exceedingly cunning, remarkably courageous in the defense of their nation, and possessed of a great affection for one another. However, as these traits were common for Mississippi river-country natives, it was often said of the Choctaws that their distinguishing characteristics were their flat heads, achieved by laying bricks on their newborns' foreheads, and their extraordinary capacity for oratory.

One of their most eloquent chieftains was Pushmataha, who, in 1814, had helped Davy Crockett and Andy Jackson win the Creek War, and who in 1820 had represented the Choctaw Nation at the Treaty of Doak's Stand and ceded 5,500,000 acres to the United States. Pushmataha stood six foot two, possessed enormous strength, and was unequaled in single combat. Dressed in his full Choctaw chieftain regalia—feathered headgear, hunting shirt fringed with beadwork, a bright shawl held in place with a silver band, silver bands on his arms, and seven crest-shaped gadgets around his neck—Pushmataha made a striking impression. Although he spoke Spanish, French, and several native dialects, it was with his English that Pushmataha defended his polygamy to the Americans. "I have two wives," he said, " because every woman is entitled to a husband. Among the Choctaws, many young braves fall in battle, and if they took only one wife, many women would go without husbands."

But it was his famous declaration on the legend of his birth, related here only in part, that, when rendered in English or Choctaw, most ably demonstrated his eloquence.

It was a long time ago; at the season when the glorious sun was pouring down his brightest, balmiest, and greatest life-giving influence; when the gay flowers, bedecked in their most glorious habiliments, were sweetest, brightest, and most numerous; when the joyous birds in full chorus were chanting their gleeful songs of life and love, and all the earth was full of inspiration; when all nature seemed to quiver in rapturous emotion. . . .

Anon, a cloud was rising in the west, a black angry threatening cloud, looming upwards and rapidly widening its scowling front. Harshly grumbling as it whirled its black folds onward, nearer and nearer, very soon it overspread the whole heavens, veiling the landscape in utter darkness and appalling uproar. It was a sweeping tornado, fringed with forked lightning, [and] thunders rolling and bellowing; the winds fiercely howled, and the solid earth trembled. In the height of this confusion and war of elements, a burning flash of fire gleamed through the black obscurity, a shattering crash, followed by a burst of terrific thunder. . . .

The sun poured down his beaming rays in their wonted brilliancy; but the vast, time-honored sylvan king, the red oak, had been shivered into fragments; its odd-shapen splinters lay widely scattered on the rain-beaten plain. Not a vestige remained. The object of its creation was accomplished, and in its place there was a new thing under the sun.

Shall I name it? Equipped and ready for battle, holding in his right hand a ponderous club, standing erect on the place of the demolished red oak, was your dauntless chief, Pushmataha.

On December 24, 1824, while at the bedside of his dying friend, Andy Jackson asked Pushmataha for his dying wish. "When I am dead," replied the Choctaw chieftain, "fire the big guns over me." He was cremated in Choctaw tradition, and his ashes were buried in the Congressional Cemetery in Washington, with an epitaph inscribed on his marker that reads: *Pushmataha, a Choctaw Chief lies here. . . . Pushmataha was a warrior of great distinction. He was wise in council, eloquent in an extraordinary degree; and on all occasions, and under all circumstances, the white man's friend.*

FROM LEFLEUR TO LEFLORE

On June 3, 1800, French-Canadian trader Louis LeFleur and his Choctaw-French bride, Rebecca Cravat (Pushmataha's great-niece), welcomed a son, Greenwood, whom they named in honor of one of LeFleur's partners. Twelve years later, they moved from the Pearl River's bluffs to a place now known as French Camp, twenty miles north of Kosciusko, where they established a tavern on the Natchez Trace. After changing his name to LeFlore and meeting with success in his newfound business, Louis befriended Maj. John Donly, the U.S. Mail carrier between Nashville and Natchez. Donly grew fond of young Greenwood, and convinced Louis to allow him to take the boy to Nashville to receive a first-class education.

During his schooling, the seventeen-year-old Greenwood fell in love with Donly's daughter, a fifteen-year-old beauty named Rosa. But Donly refused Greenwood's marriage proposal on grounds that his daughter was too young to leave home. Sometime after withdrawing his request, Greenwood asked his mentor, "What would you do if you loved someone and were forbidden to marry her?"

"I would steal away with her," Donly replied, not thinking about his own daughter.

But *Greenwood* certainly was, and he soon took Donly's advice and eloped with Rosa. They moved into a humble Mississippi log cabin shortly after their elopement, where they lived until Rosa died twelve years later. LeFlore next married Elizabeth Cody, cousin to Buffalo Bill Cody. After her death a year later, LeFlore married Rosa's younger sister, Priscilla, in 1834. Ironically, Priscilla had been born the very day Greenwood and Rosa had married back in 1818!

INDIAN GIVER

After Chief Pushmataha lost favor with the Choctaws for ceding much of their lands to the United States in the 1820 Treaty of Doak's Stand, the tribe unanimously elevated the twenty-two-year-old Greenwood LeFlore to preeminence as their most powerful chief. They eventually came to regret their decision when, ten years later, LeFlore signed the Treaty of Dancing Rabbit Creek, which ceded most of the remaining Choctaw lands. To LeFlore's credit, he had his people's best interests in mind when he signed the treaty, knowing they could no longer retain their lands by force and certain that their best future lay in adopting the white man's practices and beliefs. Remaining on their Mississippi homelands as American citizens, he counseled, was preferable to holding on to the old ways and traversing the Trail of Tears to an Oklahoma reservation.

LeFlore's tribal rivals countered that he had, in effect, taken a bribe to sign the treaty. In return for his support of the Treaty of Dancing Rabbit Creek, the government had granted him valuable Delta land, which would ultimately make him a very rich man. In response to this accusation, LeFlore posed the rhetorical question, "Which is worse, for a great government to offer a bribe, or a poor Indian to take one?" The question was never answered by the other chieftains who had opposed the treaty, for they, too, had received similarly sized tracts of land from the government.

The "poor" Indian chief soon tired of persistent Choctaw criticism and petitioned for U.S. citizenship. In 1835, his new countrymen elected him to the state legislature, and later voted him Mississippi's U.S. senator in 1841. During LeFlore's tenure in the U.S. Senate, one of his colleagues, generally known as a pompous windbag, took the custom of interspersing senatorial speeches with Latin phrases of ridiculous lengths and once rendered an entire speech in Latin. LeFlore promptly delivered an hour-long speech entirely in Choctaw, and then asked which speech was more interesting, his in Choctaw or the other senator's in Latin!

By the Civil War's outbreak, LeFlore could no longer lay claim to poverty, having amassed 15,000 acres of farmland and 400 slaves to work them. He also achieved great success in business, acquiring a store, sawmill, and steamboat in addition to his flourishing cotton empire. When the Yazoo River town of William's Landing left his cotton exposed to the weather but still required him to pay a $1 wharfage fee, the vindictive LeFlore attempted to kill the town by building his own wharf several miles upstream, at the point where the Yalobusha and Tallahatchie met to form the Yazoo. He named the town that soon grew up around his wharf Point Leflore, and spent $75,000 to construct a turnpike sufficient to lure away much of William's Landing's business. Although Point Leflore flourished for a few years, it later faded into history as William's Landing gained preeminence on the Yazoo River. Ironically, the town he had attempted to destroy was later renamed in honor of LeFlore. Today, Greenwood, county seat of Leflore County, continues to reign as the largest inland long-staple cotton market in the world.

RIVER OF DEATH

More than just a political and business leader, Greenwood LeFlore also served as his people's leading reformer. He advocated education for Indian children, the adoption of Christianity by his tribesmen, and encouraged marriage, permanent residence, and culti-vation of the soil. He outlawed the sale of liquor to his people under pain of whipping, and the first culprit to feel his lash was his very own brother-in-law. However, many of his proposed reforms angered the more tradition-oriented Choctaws, especially the changes involving the abolition of time-honored tribal customs.

LeFlore supported a fair trial for those charged with murder, whereas the Choctaws had always believed in a life for a life, whether the victim's death was intentional or acciden-tal. He succeeded in preventing one execution for an accidental death by stepping between the accused and his would-be executioners and insisting that if they must take a life, they should take his. He advocated burial by Christian sepulcher, rather than the elaborate Choctaw pole-standing ceremony. He also opposed the practice of witchcraft and sorcery, which had long been part and parcel of Choctaw life. He severely tested the Choctaws' belief that witches could not be killed by promising to personally execute the first self-proclaimed witch he encountered.

Even so, because so many of their number had succumbed to malaria, the Choctaws still believed that witches resided in the Delta, and that the Delta's largest inland river produced fogs capable of bewitching people to their deaths. Consequently, they had named it "Yazoo River," meaning River of Death. LeFlore opposed this belief both by personal oration and establishing schools throughout the tribe. Eventually, belief in witchcraft faded among LeFlore's people, and their chief gave liberally of his time, money, and energy to help his tribesmen adjust to white society's rules.

Charitable to a fault, LeFlore did not limit his kindness to his own people. Although a slave owner, he was an uncharacteristically moderate one, providing generous clothing, housing, and sustenance for his slaves. He also kept a minister and doctor on his estate to provide for their needs, allowing his slaves to marry and even honoring them with wedding feasts on those happy occasions.

Leflore County Courthouse, and Confederate monument to Fort Pemberton defenders, built on Choctaw lands once used for ritual and sacrifice

Nor did his charity stop at the white man's door. LeFlore often lent money to friends and business partners alike, and it was his loan to Paul Tulane that helped that future Louisiana philanthropist start a New Orleans merchandising career. On another occasion, upon hearing many Carrollton citizens expressing sorrow that one of their townsmen had lost his home and all his possessions to fire, LeFlore took out his checkbook, wrote a check for $100 in the man's name, and somberly declared, "I am sorry a hundred dollars worth. How much are you sorry, my friends?" The subsequent contributions rescued the Carrollton man from destitution.

SEZ YOU!

Despite their lingering resentment over his proposed reforms, the Choctaws continued to ask LeFlore's help when dealing with whites. On those occasions, their chief never failed to intercede on their behalf. The most famous of these incidents occurred when they prevailed upon him to request the removal of an incompetent Indian commissioner, John Smith. LeFlore took a nonstop carriage ride to Washington, where he was received by Pres. Andrew Jackson. After the two men failed to reach an accord, the president attempted to end the discussion by saying, "I, Andrew Jackson, president of the United States, say that the commissioner is a gentleman."

To that, LeFlore boldly replied, "I, Greenwood LeFlore, chief of the Choctaws, say that he is a liar and a damn rascal, and he shall be removed!" Jackson relented, and after presenting LeFlore with a sword and the rank of colonel, he and LeFlore became lifelong friends.

HER HAND FOR A HOUSE

Although LeFlore achieved greatness in the world of politics and business, he most impressed his Delta neighbors with his stately antebellum mansion, Malmaison. Having vowed to provide his wife Priscilla and their daughter, Rebecca Cravat, with a fine mansion befitting their stature, LeFlore commissioned a two-story white-frame palace with both French and Southern Colonial features. Massive grooved columns graced the porticos and narrow galleries ran along all sides of the house. The balconies were dressed in iron grillwork, and a dogtrot hallway divided fourteen immense rooms, most with large black Italian marble mantels.

The Louis XIV parlor was finished in gold leaf and upholstered in rich, red, brocaded damask. The room's more than thirty furnishings were valued at $10,000, including brass-inlaid candelabra, an Aubusson carpet, large gold-framed mirrors, glittering chandeliers, a tortoiseshell cabinet, brass boulework, as well as murals and linen curtains that displayed French and Swiss royal scenes. Other buildings included two carriage houses, a smokehouse, and an outdoors kitchen connected to the mansion by a lengthy gallery. The spacious, Bermuda grass-sodded lawn featured holly, oak, and sugar maple trees, as well as an enclosed area LeFlore called Deer Park, where partially tame deer cavorted to the delight of his guests.

Malmaison's architect, who had fallen in love with LeFlore's daughter Rebecca during the construction, asked for and received her hand in marriage in lieu of payment for his work. As LeFlore's granddaughter was also preparing to marry, he threw them a double wedding on the mansion's grounds, which featured a delicacy-laden table over a hundred feet long. He also made each bride a wedding gift of a 500-acre plantation and 100 slaves.

Although Greenwood and Priscilla greatly enjoyed entertaining at Malmaison in the grand Delta style, the coming of the War Between the States led to the only incident in which LeFlore failed to offer unconditional Southern hospitality to his neighbors. He bitterly opposed Mississippi's secession, advocating that the South wait until the North committed a warlike act before considering secession. When war finally came, he predicted devastating defeat for the South. And in defiant response to the South's fateful secession, LeFlore again risked popular disdain by flying the American flag over Malmaison throughout the war's duration.

In 1863, Confederate general W. S. Featherstone and his staff approached Malmaison on their way to relieve Natchez. After establishing camp near the mansion, Featherstone observed a nasty storm front fast approaching. Not wishing to spend the night in a cold, driving rainstorm, Featherstone instructed a courier to request entertainment in Malmaison for the evening. LeFlore greeted the messenger with the following reply: "Tell Featherstone I will entertain him as an old friend, but it must be distinctly understood, not as a Confederate soldier."

When thus informed, Featherstone told his officers, "Well, that is the word with the bark on. He means what he says." Featherstone's company then removed their uniforms, donned civilian clothing, and were warmly received and roundly entertained by LeFlore.

Although angry Confederates once attempted to set fire to Malmaison, loyal slaves put out the fire and the mansion survived the war. Greenwood LeFlore died on August 21, 1865, seated on his porch draped in his beloved American flag. Despite LeFlore's unpopular Union stand, his funeral was well attended by a host of former Confederates.

And although Malmaison continued to rank as one of the river country's great showplaces for over seventy-five more years, it burned to the ground in 1942, but not before many of its valuables had been transferred to the home of Carolyn Hinton, a resident of the town and county that will forever bear Greenwood LeFlore's name.

STINKING BULLET RIVER

The Noxubee River, which traverses east-central Mississippi, derives its name from a battle on its banks near Starkville, waged in 1830 between the Chakchiumas and Chickasaws. Needless to say, the Chickasaws wiped out their opponents, and the battle was so bloody the Indians named the river Oka-nahka-shua, or Stinking Bullet Water. However, this was not the first time the Noxubee's waters had been bloodied by Indian battle. The Choctaws and Creeks had participated in a terrible donnybrook on its banks in 1790, a deadly conflict that arose out of a hotly contested stickball game!

Both tribes had claimed ownership of a large pond just off the river that was home to a plethora of beavers. As beaver pelts were currently much in demand in Mobile and Pensacola, the parties decided that the pond's ownership would be decided by combat, i.e., a rousing game of Choctaw stickball. With 5,000 fans camped around the field, two teams composed of 50 players prepared to square off. With clothing, ornaments, and blankets wagered on the game's outcome, the teams played for hours, with neither side able to score a decisive victory. A final round lasted an additional two hours, after which the Creeks finally emerged victorious. Far from magnanimous victors, the Creeks unwisely began hurling insults at the Choctaws, labeling them "squaws" and even flinging a petticoat their way. A Choctaw warrior, brandishing his tomahawk, charged the Creek camp, initiating a deadly melee that lasted from sundown to sunup.

The ensuing battle, fought with guns, clubs, hatchets, and knives, left 300 warriors dead, along with a number of women who had taken up their deceased husbands' weapons to continue the fight. After burying their dead during a week of mourning, the tribes passed the peace pipe and parted company. Although the Creeks relinquished the pond to the Choctaws in the interest of fomenting peace, the Choctaws claimed that the Great Spirit's displeasure with the battle led to the beavers' abandonment of the pond.

River-country people resurrected this violent tradition two centuries later as a part of the Ole Miss-Mississippi State football rivalry, during which bench-clearing brawls accompanied many a contest for the coveted Egg Bowl Trophy. A recent pigskin brawl, like the Choctaw stickball melee, also took place in Starkville, when the two teams bloodied each other during 1997 pregame warm-ups. Then, with the State students rattling car keys near the game's end in anticipation of a home-team triumph, Ole Miss snatched victory from the jaws of defeat by scoring a last-minute touchdown and two-point conversion to gain a 15-14 win and the last available 1997 bowl invitation. Unlike the more civilized Choctaws and Creeks, Bulldog and Rebel football fans have shown no interest in ever passing the peace pipe, and the odds of either school voluntarily relinquishing the Egg Bowl Trophy are roughly equivalent to those of the United States returning Virginia to the British or Manhattan Island to the Indians, although most Southerners would undoubtedly agree to give California back to the anyone crazy enough to take it.

LOVER'S LEAP

Near Macon, Mississippi, on the bluffs of the Noxubee River, lies a spot consecrated by forbidden love in the 1830s. A Choctaw brave and a farmer's daughter fell deeply in love, but their people denied their request to marry. So they made a solemn pledge that if they could not be joined in life, they would be forever united in death. Embracing on the bluffs eighty feet above the river, the lovers said their farewells and leaped to their deaths. A lone pine tree at the edge of the precipice where the lovers leapt to their doom still serves as a monument to this star-crossed Romeo and Juliet of the Noxubee Bluffs.

THE LAST LAUGH

Historically speaking, the lower Mississippi River valley Indians fared no better at white hands than did the Native Americans inhabiting other lands stretching from the banks of the Hudson River to the North Dakota plains. Although the Chickasaws nearly defeated De Soto in 1541, the Spanish significantly thinned their population with venereal disease and chicken pox. The Spaniards also crushed the Chakchiumas in 1770 and sent the Tunicas packing to Louisiana in the 1790s. The French eradicated the Natchez in 1731 and the Yazoo in 1740, thereby convincing the coastal tribes that they'd fare better in another venue.

The remaining Chickasaws and Choctaws befriended the Americans with an eye towards peacefully living out their days on their ancestral lands. In 1795, they pitched in to help defeat the Spanish and the Creek Indians, and in 1812, supported Andrew Jackson's campaigns against the British and Creeks. The United States rewarded them by stealing their lands with one treaty after another from 1820 to 1832, when some Choctaws and most Chickasaws made their terrible journey to Oklahoma along the Trail of Tears, many dying of starvation, disease, and exposure. The Choctaws who remained in Mississippi lent their support to the Confederacy, only to be stripped of their tribal rights in the early 1900s by the victorious United States government.

According to the records of the Catholic Church, which has ministered to them for the past 300 years, as of 1993, 5,000-plus Mississippi Choctaws faced a myriad of problems, including unemployment (33 percent), poverty (24 percent), illiteracy (15 percent), no formal education (42 percent) , and alcohol abuse (78 percent). With the twenty-first century looming on the horizon, the Choctaw Nation's outlook seemed as bleak as it had for the preceding 100 years.

And then, as if conjured by their own magic, the Choctaws' fortunes changed practically overnight. The Mississippi legislature legalized casino riverboat gambling in 1990, and by 1992, gambling boats were again servicing the Mississippi River cities of Tunica, Greenville, Vicksburg, and Natchez. The industry eventually spread to the Gulf Coast, and then, in July of 1994, gaming moved inland to Philadelphia, Mississippi, to the Choctaw Indian Reservation!

Under the able leadership of Choctaw chief Phillip Martin, who brought industry and gaming to the reservation, the Silverstar Resort and Casino has since become one of Mississippi's finest resort areas, offering a five-star restaurant, Las Vegas-style entertainment, the state's best and most expensive golf courses, and a profusion of means to gamble away a fortune, including slots, poker, Caribbean Stud, Mini-Baccarat, Let-It-Ride, keno, roulette, and blackjack. Not only has the casino provided unprecedented employment opportunities for the tribesmen, it has provided income at a rumored amount of $1,000 per Choctaw family member per year. And in a final ironical twist, the reservation casino has also given the Choctaws an opportunity to turn the tables on whites and legally pick their pockets for a change!

Chapter Five

A MOST UNCIVIL WAR

Any Civil War buff could regale an audience with numerous glorious tales about the incomparable Gen. Robert E. Lee, the tenacious Gen. Stonewall Jackson, the swashbuckling cavalrymen George Armstrong Custer and J. E. B. Stuart, or the steadfast, longsuffering Abraham Lincoln. But many self-proclaimed Civil War aficionados remain unfamiliar with the stories arising from the Western Theater of that war, even though the conflicts in the West were just as crucial to the war's outcome as were those in Virginia and Pennsylvania. This is unfortunate, because Mississippi river-country Civil War stories are all the more entertaining for being populated with uniquely colorful characters who, already more flamboyant than most Americans in peacetime, took their roles in this momentous conflict to unprecedented heights of courage, humor, guile, ludicrousness, and perseverance.

Vicksburg National Military Park

HARD FEELINGS

To begin with, not everyone in the Deep South fell in with the fire-eaters, demanded immediate secession, and clamored for war. In wealthy antebellum Natchez and throughout much of the poor-white-dominated Pearl and Tombigbee river valleys, pro-Union sentiment ran high. For example, one Alcorn County Unionist, Jason Niles, recorded in his wartime diary that his fellow hill-country citizen, Jim Shuler, "shot himself . . . to keep from going to war" against the Union. Niles also copied a speech by one Joel Harvey of Pilgrim's Rest Church, who interrupted a church meeting to declare, "I have no objection to meeting and praying. That's all right enough. But I don't intend to fast and pray just because Jeff Davis tells me to do so. When they were instigating this war, they didn't call on the churches to pray them into it; and now they needn't call on them to pray 'em out of it. I don't owe allegiance to Jeff Davis or Abe Lincoln."

FREE STATE OF JONES

But it was in Mississippi's Pearl River valley/Piney Woods region, where present-day Columbia, Hattiesburg, and Laurel are located, that pro-Union sentiment, or more accurately, anti-secessionist feelings, ran the deepest. This was particularly so of Jones County, which seceded from the Confederacy during the Civil War. Jones Countians had voted 376 to 24 against secession, and when their delegate to the state Secession Convention voted against their will, they hanged him in effigy on the Ellisville Courthouse steps.

Even so, many of them joined the Confederate Army and served with distinction until their new nation passed the Twenty Negro Law, which excused from military service men owning twenty or more slaves so they could return home and help manage their large estates. Convinced now that their cause was little more than a "rich man's war and a poor man's fight," many Jones Countians deserted Confederate ranks and went back to their homes. Within a few months, over a hundred of them had joined up with a former Confederate officer-turned-renegade named Newt Knight.

Tall, dark-haired, and handsome, Knight also possessed "cold, hard eyes [that] could whither an opponent before a blow was ever struck." He and his men holed up on a Leaf River island called "Devil's Den," and from there waged successful guerilla warfare against "trespassing" Confederates and Federals attempting to requisition horses, beef, and other supplies. Knight's charges communicated with each other via homemade hunting horns, and they utilized this unusual communication strategy and their exceptional knowledge of the local terrain to frustrate their opponents. And when the Confederacy sent Maj. Amos McLemore to capture him in 1863, Knight boldly strode up to McLemore's camp, shot the major dead, and escaped into the woods. Knight's band, known as "The Republic of Jones," eventually acquired such a terrifying reputation that, when they once approached a Jones County Confederate POW camp, the Rebel defenders armed their Yankee prisoners to aid in defense of the fort, and the Union prisoners gladly pitched in and defended their own prison camps against Knight's raiders!

Never captured, Knight survived the war and lived to the ripe old age of ninety-two. Not surprisingly, he became a leading figure in Jones County politics during the Reconstruction era.

THE STAR THAT SET ON GRANT

On the other hand, the Mississippi river-country inhabitants who supported the "War for Southern Independence" gave the Confederacy many great victories against overwhelming odds. One came at the Battle of Fort Pemberton, fought just outside present-day Greenwood on the banks of the Tallahatchie River. And the principal character in that drama was a ship appropriately named the *Star of the West*.

Originally commissioned as a New York City merchant vessel, the *Star of the West* was built by Commodore Cornelius Vanderbilt in 1861 at a cost of $250,000. But when Confederates seized Fort Sumter in Charleston, President Lincoln sent the Union merchant vessel to Charleston loaded with supplies, four officers, and 250 artillerymen and marines. Although Lincoln attempted to pass her off as a civilian trade vessel, a Southern correspondent working in Washington cabled his Charleston newspaper's publisher about the vessel's actual cargo. "Blow the *Star of the West* out of the water" was the Confederate brass's directive to the Charleston commander upon discovering Lincoln's intentions.

When the *Star* attempted to slip into Charleston, the Confederates fired across her bow and chased her from the harbor. This was the first time the American flag received gunfire from Southern secessionists, and it led to a bloody four-year war between the states.

Lincoln later sent the *Star of the West* to the Gulf of Mexico for transport duty. One day, her captain, John McGowan, was scouting along the Texas shoreline near Indianola when Confederate general Earl Van Dorn and two lieutenants boarded his ship and demanded its surrender.

"You'll never get it," responded McGowan, as his soldiers made ready their defenses.

"You have three minutes to make your choice," replied a confident Van Dorn. "I have a heavy force of men and guns concealed in the bushes on shore. Unless you surrender all your forces, I'll have you blown to hell!"

Believing that Confederate soldiers lurked behind every shoreline bush, McGowan surrendered his vessel and led his disarmed charges ashore.

"Now you are on land," Van Dorn said to his opponents. "Go where you damn well please."

"But aren't you going to furnish us with military escort for safety?" asked McGowan, casting about for the full body of the rebel force.

"Safety, hell," laughed the reb leader. "You surrendered your ship and men to three Confederates. We have no forces concealed." The three rebels promptly sailed the Star of the West to New Orleans, where she received a Confederate refitting as a Mississippi River gunboat.

Shortly thereafter, General Grant began his back-door invasion of Vicksburg. Seeking a safe route to the heavily defended "Gibraltar of the Confederacy," Grant passed his fleet, consisting of three ironclads and two transports loaded with 6,000 troops, through Moon Lake and Yazoo Pass, down the Coldwater River, and then into the Tallahatchie River. From there he intended to float his ships down to Greenwood, where the Tallahatchie and Yalobusha rivers joined to form the Yazoo River. It was then a simple matter of floating downriver and striking Vicksburg from the rear.

Warned by Southern spies of the flotilla's progression into Moon Lake, Gen. William W. Loring, a few civil engineers, 200 slaves, and 1,500 civilians hastily constructed a breast-work of logs, fence rails, sandbags, and cotton bales on a patch of land three miles above Greenwood. The spot was chosen because it overlooked a bend in the Tallahatchie where the river was only wide enough to accommodate one boat at a time. Three hundred yards upriver from the hastily erected and newly christened Fort Pemberton, the Confederates positioned the *Star of the West* in midstream. Her captain, Lt. A. A. Stoddard, ordered the crew to drill 250 holes in her below-water hull and plug them with oak bungs. Then they waited for Grant's armada to arrive.

Site of Fort Pemberton battle, Greenwood

At 10:00 A.M., on March 11, 1863, the Union fleet, under the command of Gen. L. R. Ross, appeared on the river, a few miles west of Greenwood. The Confederates pulled the *Star of the West's* plugs and she sank to the bottom, her masts protruding ominously above the Tallahatchie's waves. When the Federals began their attack, rebel sharpshooters and their lone cannon treated their opponents to a frightful, hot-shell reception. As one Confederate later reported, the Yanks "met with such a warm reception from our cannon planted along the south bank of the Tallahatchie . . . that they were glad to retire."

But the Federals returned on March 13 and an all-day battle ensued. "Give 'em the blizzards, boys," shouted General Loring, and his men rained shot down upon the Union fleet. Unable to land his men because of springtime flooding, Ross again retreated. On March 16, the Federals returned for one more battle, but the Confederates prevailed in less than twenty minutes, fully incapacitating the Union gunboat, *Chillicothe.* All told, the rebels suffered less than a dozen casualties compared to thirty-one Yankee wounded or dead. When apprized of the stunning Confederate victory at Greenwood, Grant abandoned his backside approach to Vicksburg and made plans to take Vicksburg by land. To this day, Greenwood youths still plumb the Tallahatchie's depths in search of what remains of the *Star of the West,* the ship that sank Grant's Tallahatchie assault.

IMMACULATE DEFLECTION

Grant ultimately decided to approach Vicksburg via land by debarking at Port Gibson and driving through Raymond and Jackson. On their overland march, Grant's forces burned Jackson, thereby earning that city the unfortunate wartime nickname of "Chimneyville," since little of its buildings survived apart from charred, smoldering chimneys. The battle that paved Grant's way into Jackson was the Battle of Raymond, which took place west of Jackson near the Big Black River. During that battle, the most unusual event of the war in Mississippi occurred.

Dr. L. G. Capers, a Confederate surgeon, treated a young man for a bullet wound to his scrotum that had destroyed his left testicle. Moments later he treated a young woman's injuries caused by a bullet to her abdomen. Although both wounds were of the sort that usually proved fatal in the mid-1800s, both parties achieved a full recovery. When Dr. Capers returned to Raymond six months later, he was surprised to find the same young lady in an advanced state of pregnancy. Two hundred and seventy-eight days after receiving her wounds, the woman delivered an eight-pound baby boy. She later surprised Capers even further by swearing to him that she was a virgin who had enjoyed no sexual relations of any kind prior to becoming pregnant!

Three weeks later, when examining the baby boy, Capers removed a metal object from its scrotum, part of a mashed Yankee Minié ball. Astonished by his discovery, Dr. Capers explained to the woman's family that the ball had passed through the young man's testicle, "carrying with it particles of semen into the abdomen of the young lady, then through her left ovary, and into the uterus, in this manner impregnating her!"

Although skeptical at first, the young gentleman ultimately agreed to visit the new mother and, upon discovering a distinct resemblance between himself and the infant, agreed to marry her four months after the child's birth. The improbable couple later gave birth to two other children, and Dr. Capers' account of the miraculous birth was published in *The American Medical Weekly* in 1874.

MOON OVER THE MISSISSIPPI

Surrounded by potential enemies and insurrectionists, the conquering Northerners often resorted to stern measures when dealing with rebellious citizens. Benjamin ("Beast") Butler, who ruled New Orleans with an iron hand, hanged one citizen for insulting the American flag, treated women who insulted Yankee soldiers as prostitutes, arrested all who displayed Confederate flags or wore mourning black, and even imprisoned one woman for greeting a Union soldier's funeral procession with the comment, "There goes one Yankee, and I'd like to see a lot more of them going the same way!" Admiral Farragut ended Baton Rouge insurrectionist activity by shelling the city, killing three citizens and wounding three more. But the Yanks weren't able to silence every act of reb resistance.

According to historian Jim Miles, during Grant's conquest of the Mississippi River town Grand Gulf, one citizen fired his pistol at passing Union ironclads from a vantage on the river's bluffs. The ships shelled him in response, and as the bombs burst around him, the fellow turned his back, dropped his pants, and patted his rear end.

IRONCLAD DISAGREEMENT

Every American elementary student studied the immortal battle between the Civil War ironclads, the *Monitor* and the *Merrimack,* and most can recall the strange, submarine-like appearance of the two metal-covered ships. Less well known, but perhaps of greater consequence to the outcome of the war, were the ironclad battles on the Mississippi and Yazoo rivers. In one battle, a lone Southern ironclad almost destroyed the whole of the Union's Mississippi River fleet, single-handedly blunting one of Grant's early assaults on Vicksburg. Outfitted with five cannon and constructed with an armor-plated pilothouse and smokestack atop a casemated gun deck, the *Arkansas* weighed 1,000 tons, cost $77,000 to build, and could travel four miles an hour against the Mississippi's mighty current.

With a purpose of single-handedly rescuing Vicksburg from the whole of the Union fleet, she left her Yazoo City port on July 15, 1862 and steamed for the Mississippi River. Along the way, her commander, Lt. Isaac N. Brown, stopped and asked information of a slave concerning the enemy's whereabouts. The slave refused to answer on grounds that he would not give information to a Yankee. "Look at my uniform," argued Brown. "Can you not see it is gray?"

"Sure you are a Yankee," the slave boldly replied. "We don't have any of those gunboats."

While still on the Yazoo, the *Arkansas* met three Union ships, the ironclad *Carondolet,* the tinclad *Tyler,* and the ramming ship *Queen of the West,* all sent by Admiral Farragut to intercept her. She ran the Union ironclad aground in flames and so terrorized the other two ships that they retreated in panic to Vicksburg. "The *Arkansas* is coming; the *Arkansas* is coming," yelled their terrified crews as they arrived at the Union fleet stationed below the Bluff City.

When she finally turned a bend and had Vicksburg in view, the already wounded *Arkansas* encountered "a forest of [Federal] masts and smokestacks, sloops, rams, iron-clads and other gunboats." Faced with five Union ironclads, seven rams, a man-of-war, and various gunboats, the valiant *Arkansas* steamed full ahead and engaged every ship on the river. Taking continuous shots from all sides as she plowed through the enemy fleet, the *Arkansas* disabled several ships and forced many others to turn tail and flee. Although Lieutenant Brown lost half his crew, he broke through to Vicksburg, leaving seventeen Union dead and forty-two Yankee sailors injured in his wake. Vicksburgers cheered the incredible victory and enjoyed a four-month respite during the enemy fleet's withdrawal to New Orleans. Enraged at the humiliation his fleet had incurred at the hands of the *Arkansas,* however, Admiral Farragut immediately ordered the vessel's destruction.

His chance came sooner than expected as the *Arkansas* charged downriver several days later. Even after her engines broke down a few miles short of Baton Rouge, the Federal fleet cautiously hung back while Brown ordered the *Arkansas* scuttled by her own men. In light of the devastating effect of one humble ironclad on the Union fleet, some scholars have blamed the Confederate loss of Vicksburg upon rebel leaders' failure to get the other ironclads up and running in time to engage the Federal fleet on the Mississippi.

In any event, a crippling blow was dealt the Confederate Navy by Union lieutenant commander John Walker's sinking of three under-construction ironclads in a Yazoo River navy yard near Yazoo City. The *Mobile, Republic,* and another as-yet-unnamed Confederate ironclad that measured 310 feet in length and sported four-inch iron armor and four engines were destroyed at dry dock by Walker in 1863. Had he not sunk these Confederate ironclads, they may have successfully defended Vicksburg against Grant's entire naval force.

FOOLED YOU!

But perhaps the war's most interesting ironclad battle was one that involved no battle at all and really didn't even involve opposing ironclads. The event occurred in 1863 and may constitute the greatest deception ever perpetrated during the Civil War. Upon hearing that the Confederates were attempting to salvage a damaged ironclad, the *Indianola,* which was grounded on the Mississippi near Vicksburg, Capt. William Porter devised a scheme to trick the Confederates into surrender. He dressed up an old flatboat with canvas and wood to resemble an ironclad. Porter's "ironclad" flew a skull and crossbones flag over her deck, and on her fake paddle wheel she displayed the words *Deluded People Cave In.* The ship took twelve hours to build at a cost of $8.63, but when the rebels repairing the *Indianola* saw her steaming downriver toward them, they abandoned their wounded vessel, tossing several cannon in the river and exploding many others. Writing about his clever tactic after the war, Porter noted that if the *Monitor*'s captain had saved his country with an iron ship, there was no reason why he couldn't "save it with a wooden one."

VICKSBURGERS ON A SILVER PLATTER

The greatest river battle of the war took place at Vicksburg after Grant finally fought his way to the Bluff City on May 19, 1863. Grant was very pleased to begin this fight, having already suffered several failed attempts to bring his army and fleet to Vicksburg. In addition to the failed Tallahatchie back-door ploy, he had constructed a canal to reroute the Mississippi away from Vicksburg and leave that city high and dry, but a rapid rise in the river flooded his canal and doomed that scheme. But with the river controlled by his navy and all Confederate ironclads reduced to a memory, Grant believed the end was in sight after his troops had fought their way to Vicksburg through Raymond, Jackson, and Champion's Hill. Shortly after his arrival at Vicksburg in May, Grant instituted regular bombardments of the city, designed to weary the Confederate troops and diminish the populace's morale.

Finally, on May 22, 1863, the Union commander ordered his fleet to shell the city for several hours before launching an all-out infantry assault. The rebels soundly squashed this attack, with Grant's force of 40,000 suffering 3,199 casualties, while General Pemberton's defenders, 20,000 strong, suffered a mere 500 killed or wounded. Grant promptly dug in his heels and besieged the city for the next forty-seven days and nights.

Although opposing troops passed much of the siege time exchanging jokes, stories, coffee, liquor, and tobacco, the siege created a living hell for the townspeople, reducing them to dining on mule, rat, and pea-meal bread and forcing them to carve out hillside caves to avoid the endless shelling.

Two stories illustrate the effect upon its recipients of the unnerving, continuous bombardment. A visiting Northerner, trapped in the town with his Southern relatives, observed what appeared to him to be the fuse of a mortar shell descending upon him. He dove under his wagon, peered out, and, realizing that the spark was coming closer, got out and danced a panicked jig, vainly attempting to get out from under its path of descent. "Darn the thing!" he finally exclaimed. "Why don't it bust?" After observing this spectacle for a full minute, a passerby informed the visitor that he had been dodging a lightning bug!

Another terrified soul, a French Confederate engineer oft driven to distraction by the howling and bursting of shells, suffered frequent ribbing by his fellow engineers for his skittishness during mortar bombardments. "I no like ze bomb," he unabashedly explained. "I cannot fight him back."

The siege, terrible though it was, never completely blunted the Southern fighting spirit. When on July 3 Pemberton and Grant met to discuss terms of surrender, and Grant offered his customary terms of unconditional surrender, Pemberton replied, "We will go to fighting again at once. I can assure you, you will bury many more of your men before you enter Vicksburg." Grant quickly offered better terms, and Vicksburg fell into Union hands.

History records that Grant's river-country conquest was more the result of Southern incompetence than Yankee ingenuity. Pres. Jefferson Davis apparently made a poor choice in Pemberton as Vicksburg's champion, since the man possessed little previous experience in the field. Pemberton also incurred a lion's share of the blame by failing to marshal his forces and attack Grant at a time when success may have followed, and by losing his army in a city that he probably should have abandoned as hopeless to defend. Gen. Joseph E. Johnston also did his part to lose Vicksburg by failing to follow Davis's order to relieve Pemberton in June by attacking Grant's flank and placing him between two hostile forces, which, counted together, outnumbered Grant's troops.

Perhaps Vicksburger Emma Balfour stated it best when asked by Gen. Stephen Lee during the siege if she had prepared a rathole sufficient to shield herself from the shelling. "It seemed to me," she replied, "we were all caught in a rathole." She might have added that the rats commanding the Confederate defense of the Bluff City had served Vicksburgers and their courageous defenders up to Grant on a platter forged of hesitancy, insubordination, and ineptitude.

WHAT A RELIEF!

Grant's path to Vicksburg proved the rockiest of roads; he faced fierce rebel resistance along the way, endured a shaky relationship with the Northern press, and suffered a few notorious rounds with the bottle. And as if all this were not trouble enough, Grant frequently faced dissension among his ranks. His chief dissenter was the politically well connected but largely ineffective Gen. John A. McClernand. McClernand once refused to obey Grant's battlefield order and added insult to injury by cursing Grant in front of the messenger, engineering officer Col. James Wilson. When Wilson responded to the insult by saying, "I will pull you off that horse and beat the boots off of you," McClernand assured Wilson that he meant no insult but was "simply expressing [his] intense vehemence on the subject matter." Amused by word of McClernand's temper tantrum, Grant later excused another of his general's outbursts by saying, "He is not cursing. He is simply expressing his intense vehemence on the subject." Nevertheless, Grant determined to find an acceptable basis for canning the troublesome McClernand.

His opportunity came a few days later when McClernand violated military protocol by releasing a story to the press lauding his own personal accomplishments during Grant's

Statue of U. S. Grant, Vicksburg National Military Park

unsuccessful May 22 assault on Vicksburg. As Grant prepared to deliver a letter of dismissal to McClernand, Colonel Wilson not only volunteered to relay the order, he set out to do so in the wee hours of the morning so McClernand wouldn't have time to redeem himself with a victory the next morning. Upon receiving Grant's dismissal order from Wilson at 2:00 A.M., McClernand said, "Well, sir! I am relieved." The delighted Wilson exclaimed, "By God, sir, we are both relieved!"

TRUE FEMME FATALES

While Southern ladies supported the "Cause" with extraordinary perseverance, high spirits, and even by forming "Needle Regiments" to sew uniforms for their rebellious heroes, Northern women actually took up arms and joined fighting regiments in support of the United States during the Vicksburg campaign, although no one knew it at the time. Pvt. Albert Cashier of the Ninety-fifth Illinois, "the smallest man in the company," was considered by his mates to be "unusually quiet and reclusive, but a good soldier" and was not discovered to be a woman named Jenny Hodgers until years after the war.

Another fighting femme, Almeda Hart, enlisted in the U.S. Army under the name of James Strong when her husband left her behind in Memphis to join Grant's Vicksburg campaign. She served as a Union courier and her deception was not discovered until a century later, when historians discovered one of her letters to her mother, which read, "You would be surprised if you were to see me for I have turned from Henry Hart's wife to a nice young man."

Illinois Monument, Vicksburg National Military Park

HAVE A SODA AND A GRIMACE

Unwilling to do without many of the conveniences of civilized society simply because a bloody war raged in their own backyards, inventive Confederate ladies fashioned original recipes and designs to meet their basic needs and desires. These included

coffee	parched corn and okra or dried sweet potatoes
tea	dried raspberry leaves and water
soda	sour milk or vinegar mixed with lye burnt out of corncobs
for a snack	mixed nuts, e.g., acorns and pecans
wax candles	quicklime and mutton suet
ink and dyes	berries and tree bark
horse collars	plaited corn shucks
hats	palmetto leaves
for nausea	peach-tree leaves and water
for cough	tar and honey

In light of these creative adjustments, it must surely be conceded that, if necessity is the mother of invention, then Southern mothers are the best answer to necessity.

ASS A LA CARTE

The siege of Vicksburg worked a nightmarish devilment upon Vicksburg's citizenry. Residing in underground caves to avoid Union shells, the people dined upon pea-meal bread, horses, mules, dogs, cats, and, at last resort, rats. They nevertheless managed to keep their sense of humor, using tombstones as dining tables and quaffing ginger beer to slake their thirst. They even circulated a pamphlet that read:

> Parties arriving by the river or Grant's inland route will find Grape, Canister & Co.'s carriages at the landing or any Depot on the line of entrenchments. Buck and Ball Co. take charge of all baggage. No effort will be spared to make the visit of all as interesting as possible.

Confederate soldiers also got in on the act, inventing an 1863 menu for a fictitious "Hotel de Vicksburg." After his commander had issued an order to select the fattest mules for slaughter, Confederate major Eugene S. Bolling barely managed to rescue his superior's favorite mule, Morgan, from the army's slaughterhouse. As a memorial to the incident, Major Bolling presented the following bill of fare to his grateful commander, which later found its way throughout the besieged city and even into Union lines, from whence it appeared in several Northern newspapers:

HOTEL De VICKSBURG
[Drawing of mule's head and hand holding knife]
BILL OF FARE
SOUP

Mule Tail

SIDE DISHES

Mule Salad
Mule Hoof soused
Mule Brains a la Omelette
Mule Kidney stuffed with Peas
Mule Tripe fried in Pea Meal batter
Mule Tongue cold a la bray

JELLIES

Mule Foot

PASTRY

Pea Meal Pudding blackberry sauce
Cotton Seed Pies
Chinaberry Tarts

DESSERT

White Oak Acorns
Beech Nuts
Blackberry Leaf Tea
Genuine Confederate Coffee

LIQUORS
Mississippi Water vintage 1492 Superior
Lime Stone Water late importation very fine
Spring Water Vicksburg brand
Waul Legion Well very pure

Meals at all hours; gentlemen wait upon themselves; any inattention on the part of servants will be promptly reported at the office.

Jeff Davis & Co.
Proprietors

Miraculously, old Morgan survived both the siege and the war, for which he was given the new name, "Morgan Escape."

SARTORIUS OR SARTORIOUS?

Some 250,000 Jews traded their Central European life of religious persecution for a second chance in America during the early to mid-1800s. After enduring a month-long steerage-class boat ride to the New World, a substantial number of them settled in the Mississippi river country. Finding acceptance and hospitality to their liking, many made significant contributions to the Confederacy's wartime effort. Little Rosalie Beckham was Natchez's sole Civil War casualty, while Judah P. Benjamin ably served successively as the Confederacy's attorney general, secretary of war, and secretary of state.

The most unusual tale of Civil War Jewry concerns Philip Sartorious, the first rebel soldier to suffer wounds in the defense of Vicksburg. Although his physicians assured him that his wounds were mortal, Sartorious sufficiently recovered to father *nineteen children* during his fifty-six-year marriage to Sophie Rose! This may have been what Mr. Faulkner had in mind when he spoke of not only enduring, but prevailing!

NEITHER RAIN, NOR SNOW, NOR DEEP OF RIVER

Even the bloodiest war in the Western Hemisphere couldn't interrupt river-country mail service, and no one did more to ensure the mail's continued delivery than Ab Grymes, Confederate mailman. With the Mississippi River as his route, Grymes carried the mail to Confederates at all points between St. Louis and Vicksburg. His job became all the more hazardous after the Federals controlled the river, with the reality that his capture would land him on the wrong end of a Yankee firing squad. But Ab Grymes never let the Union navy keep him from his duly appointed tasks.

His daring exploits were numerous, but his most famous occurred in May of 1863, when he devised a rather extraordinary means to run the Federal gauntlet and bring the mail to besieged Vicksburg defenders. For this assignment, Grymes placed the mail in four water-tight metal boxes, and he and his companion, Bob Loudon, wired the boxes and a pair of oars inside a partially submerged skiff. Clinging to the craft's sides in the Mississippi's chilly waters, the two paddled their way to Vicksburg using frying pans. After passing by the Union gunboats, they bailed water with the frying pans, climbed aboard, and rowed into the city. After making their delivery, Grymes and Loudon fastened the return mail boxes to the bottom of their boat, donned Union uniforms, and rowed past the unwitting Yankees in broad daylight!

NEVER SAY NEVER

Although the forty-seven-day siege of Vicksburg is the more well known battle, the forty-eight-day siege of Port Hudson, Louisiana, 200 river miles south of Vicksburg, was just as spectacular a conflict. With 6,340 rebels defending against 16,000 Yankees, the match seemed lopsided at first, but the well-entrenched Confederates put up a memorable struggle in a battle that pitted perhaps the South's best sharpshooters against one of the North's bravest regiments, the black troops of Gen. Nathaniel P. Banks.

As was the case at Vicksburg, the Yanks first attempted to take the town by storm. The first Federal assault cost 2,000 casualties compared to 235 Confederate losses, while the second resulted in 1,800 Union and only 47 Confederate killed or wounded. Banks' forces promptly laid siege to the fort, with the 200 Port Hudson citizens suffering even worse privation than did besieged Vicksburgers. In perhaps the world's best example of adding insult to injury, Yankee soldiers, after discovering that the rebels had been reduced to dining on mules, perched themselves on the Mississippi's banks and brayed like mules at their starving opponents. But despite all their troubles, Port Hudson's defenders bravely held out until five days after the fall of Vicksburg, which had left their position untenable.

Ironically, Franklin Gardner, the Confederate commander at Port Hudson, was, like Vicksburg's Pemberton, a reconstructed Northerner, and their mutual nemesis, Adm. David Farragut, was born and bred a Southerner. Such Civil War ironies were legion; the state of Missouri furnished seventeen Confederate and twenty-two Union regiments to the Battle of Vicksburg.

Another striking example of wartime irony concerns Port Hudson defender Jim Fraiser and Vicksburg Confederate Francis Marion Howard. Private Fraiser was taken prisoner on July 9, 1863, took an oath of allegiance to the Union shortly thereafter, and was released the next day on parole. He later defended against General Sherman's drive through Georgia to the sea. Private Howard, descended from one Revolutionary War hero and named after another, also took the oath of Union allegiance after Vicksburg's fall and was paroled on July 10, only to continue his Confederate service under General Bragg during the siege of Chattanooga. Both men survived numerous campaigns, and, although they never met, Fraiser's grandson married Howard's granddaughter, who gave birth to John James Fraiser, Jr., who faithfully served the United States as a decorated World War II, B-24 top-turret gunner over Germany and Italy! Sergeant Fraiser completed his family's circle of allegiance, revolt, and regained fealty when, in 1996, he was elected Mississippi's first court of appeal's chief justice and took an oath to defend the laws of the same nation that his Revolutionary forefathers had fought to establish and that his Confederate forebears had fervently attempted to dissolve!

WANTED: YANKEE KILLERS!

While the Civil War's Eastern Theater showcased many dashing generals and courageous cavalrymen such as J. E. B. Stuart, George A. Custer, and John Mosby's Virginia Raiders, warfare in the West produced the most intriguing and by far the greatest fighter of them all—Nathan Bedford Forrest. Having grown up hard in the tough backcountry of south-central Tennessee and northern Mississippi, Forrest, by successfully dealing in land, cattle, cotton, and slaves, had emerged as a Memphis millionaire by the Civil War's outbreak. Although he entered Confederate service as a private, his exploits soon resulted in a meteoric rise to a lieutenant general's rank. Forrest's wartime philosophy may be best summed up by three of his most famous sayings: "get there the fustest with the mostest," "shoot at everything blue and keep the skeer [scare] on," and "war means fightin', and fightin' means killin'." He was nothing if not a fighter and a killer, and is believed to have personally slain over thirty Yankee soldiers and to have had at least twenty-nine horses shot out from under him.

Forrest developed a then-revolutionary strategy of utilizing his calvary as "mounted infantry," swiftly moving his men to a battleground, then dispatching them on foot, armed with as many pistols as they could carry. Such tactics eventually made Forrest the most feared Confederate general on the Western front.

And he came by that reputation honestly, often personally leading his men into battle. Frustrated with what he perceived to be the overcautious nature of his superiors at Shiloh, Forrest, with his bloodlust raging and his steed galloping at a breakneck pace, outdistanced his men and found himself surrounded by Northern infantry. As the Federals closed ranks around him, he hacked his way through them with his saber, and after a Union infantryman shot him in the back, Forrest repaid the man with a fatal sword blow. Forrest then reached down, grabbed another Yank by the collar, pulled him ahorse, and used him as a shield from Union gunfire as he galloped back to his brigade!

While recovering from wounds received at Shiloh, Forrest ran a newspaper ad designed to attract new recruits for his regiment, which provided a marvelous insight into his future intentions:

200 Recruits Wanted!

I will receive 200 able-bodied men if they will present themselves at my headquarters by the first of June with good horse and gun. I wish none but those who desire to be actively engaged. My headquarters for the present is at Corinth, Miss. Come on boys, if you want a heap of fun and to kill some Yankees.

N.B. Forrest
Colonel, Commanding
Forrest's Regiment

CAN'T SEE THE REBELS FOR THE FORREST

Forrest never lost a battle until the waning days of the war, and his most impressive victories came in the Mississippi river country in 1864. By the mid-1860s several important towns had cropped up along the Tombigbee River in northeast Mississippi from Tupelo to Columbus. It was near two of these, Okolona and Baldwyn, that Forrest earned the victories that have made his tactics required study in military academies throughout the world.

Having determined that the war in the West could not be won until Forrest had been eliminated, General Sherman had assigned Brig. Gen. William Sooy Smith the task of finding and destroying Forrest's regiment in north Mississippi. On February 21, 1864, the two generals' forces met in the sleepy little town of West Point, a few miles west of the Tombigbee. Shortly after Forrest's 2,500 troops engaged Smith's 5,000, Smith realized that he had bitten off more than he could chew. When the Yankees turned tail and headed for Memphis, Forrest chased them all the way to Okolona. Whenever the Federals paused to cross the Tombigbee or any other stream, Forrest dismounted his men and sent them charging into the Union line with pistols blazing.

The fleeing Yankees showed good sense in continuing their flight; Forrest shot four soldiers and sabered another who foolishly turned to face him. The very sight of Forrest terrified his enemies, for Forrest "never seemed to touch his saddle, but stood up in his stirrups, an attitude which gave him the appearance of being a foot taller than he really was," as Confederate colonel Barteau explained. "As he was over six feet in stature and of large proportions, and of necessity rode a large horse, so it was not difficult to recognize his imposing presence at any ordinary distance along the line."

At Okolona, the Federals, armed with breechloading rifles, made another stand, girded by their superior numbers and weapons and buoyed by their legendary calvary leader, Brig. Gen. Benjamin Greirson, who had earlier made a famous raid through Mississippi. Like Smith, Grierson proved no match for the Wizard of the Saddle, and the rebels soon had their blue-clad foes on the run. After growing tired of running, the Federals finally turned to make a charge of their own from the heart of downtown Okolona. Just at the time when his Confederates realized that they were about to face a "cornered bear," Forrest seized the moment, dashed to the fore, lifted his hat, and politely said, "Mount your horses." When advised that the enemy was marshaling a charge, Forrest declared, "Then we will charge *them.*" The Confederates galloped down two of Okolona's streets and opened fire 150 yards from the Federal line. As the enemy panicked, broke, ranks and fled, Forrest led his charge right over the fleeing Federals.

Forrest harassed the Union army most of the way back to Memphis. Personally leading charge after charge, Forrest had two horses shot out from under him and, after refusing a doctor's request to retire from the most dangerous area of the battle, grabbed a rifle and led another charge on foot. The Yanks made one final stand at Pontotoc, offering what Forrest later described as "one of the grandest cavalry charges I have ever witnessed." It did them no good, however, and Forrest's men put a "skeer" on Billy Yank that lasted all the way to downtown Memphis.

THE WIZARD AT THE CROSSROADS

Four months later, the Battle of Brices Cross Roads, several miles up the Tombigbee from Okolona, earned Forrest's tactics martial history's highest accolades. These tactics included (1) never holding back reserves, but hitting the enemy with all available forces on each charge, (2) for the first time in history, ordering an artillery command to charge without the support of accompanying cavalry or infantry, with specific orders to "charge right down the road . . . get [the cannon] as close as you can," and "give 'em hell," and (3) swiftly positioning men armed with navy six-shooters for hand-to-hand combat with the enemy, because the Federals, armed with repeating rifles, enjoyed a long-range advantage over the single-shot-rifle-toting Southerners, but lost that advantage at close quarters when Southern pistols faced Northern sabers.

Making maximum use of the home-field advantage was another of Forrest's successful stratagems, and he employed it to great effect at Brices Cross Roads. Prior to the engagement, Forrest told his officers how he believed his 2,000 Confederates would defeat 8,000 Federals.

> I know they greatly outnumber the troops I have at hand, but the road along which they will march is narrow and muddy; they will make slow progress. The country is densely wooded and the undergrowth so heavy that when we strike them they will not know how few men we have.
>
> Their cavalry will move ahead of their infantry and should reach the crossroads three hours in advance. We can whip their cavalry in that time. As soon as the fight opens they will send back to have the infantry hurried up. It is going to be hot as hell, and coming on a run for five or six miles, their infantry will be so tired out we will ride right over them.

As usual, Forrest's plan worked to perfection, and as had been the case at Okolona, a Southern-fried Yankee rout was in the making. As the Confederates chased the Union troops back to Memphis at 3:00 A.M. on June 11, 1864, Forrest giddily exclaimed, "Keep the skeer on 'em!" When a wagon overturned in Tishomingo Creek, the Federal retreat turned to panic, and their entire force would have suffered annihilation but for the bravery and cover fire of black wagon-guard troops. After the Rebels chased the fleeing Yankees fifty miles to La Grange, Tennessee, the federals counted 2,165 casualties compared to Forrest's 492.

Angered over this latest humiliation, Sherman sent Lincoln word that he was ordering two Union generals "from Memphis to pursue and kill Forrest." Sherman added that the Southern "devil" Forrest must be "hunted down and killed if it costs 10,000 lives and bankrupts the [national] treasury!"

YOUR LUGGAGE IS BEING HELD PRISONER IN THE LOBBY

The last assignment any Union general wanted was one that placed him directly in Bedford Forrest's path. For Sherman's two commissioned Forrest hunters, being in the wrong place at the right time proved their only defense against the notorious rebel cavalryman.

Shortly after his resounding victory at Brices Cross Roads, Forrest determined to press his advantage and make a surprise raid on Memphis, which had been in Federal hands for the past two years. Around 4:00 a.m., the Confederates charged into Memphis down the Hernando road giving a terrifying "rebel yell." Bill Forrest, Bedford's brother, rode right into the lobby of Gayoso House Hotel (not the Peabody Hotel, as is widely believed), where General Hulbert was reportedly lodged, but the general had luckily taken up residence

Statue of N. B. Forrest, Biloxi

elsewhere for the evening. Forrest's other kinsman, Lt. Col. Jesse Forrest, made a run at General Washburn's headquarters, but the Union general, dressed only in his nightgown, escaped by foot to Fort Pickering a half-mile away. The rebels satisfied themselves by taking Washburn's uniform as their prisoner.

After the raid, Hulbert made one of the war's most celebrated comments. "They removed me from command," Hulbert groused, "because I couldn't keep Forrest out of west Tennessee. And now Washburn can't keep him out of his own bedroom!"

FORGET, HELL!

Greenville's noted Civil War historian and acclaimed novelist Shelby Foote contacted Bedford Forrest's granddaughter while preparing his notes for Ken Burns' PBS series "The Civil War." When Foote informed her that he believed that the conflict produced two "authentic geniuses"—Abraham Lincoln and her grandfather—the lady grew silent for a moment, and then replied, "Well, you know, in our family, we never thought much of Mr. Lincoln."

VENGEANCE IS THE LORD'S, BELIEVE IT OR NOT

Founded in 1765 and incorporated in 1828, the Mississippi River town Rodney had 4,000 residents by 1860 and was one of Mississippi's most prosperous cotton towns. The pride of the community was the Presbyterian Church, built in 1829 as a red brick structure with rounded arches and a stepped gable leading to an octagonal bell tower. On Sunday morning, September 13, 1863, the Rodney Presbyterian Church held its usual services with the presence of some unusual guests—much of the crew of the Federal tinclad Rattler. The Rattler had earlier met defeat at the Battle of Fort Pemberton near Greenwood and, after the fall of Vicksburg, had been assigned patrol duty of Mississippi River waters near Vicksburg. Finding the Rattler anchored near his church, Reverend Baker had courteously invited her crew to hear one of his sermons.

With the *Rattler*'s captain and crew engaged in singing the second hymn of the day, a band of Confederate scouts burst through the doors and demanded the Federals' surrender. They took most of the *Rattler*'s crew prisoner, except one seaman, whose local girlfriend hid him in folds of her skirt and undergarments as she sat quietly on a pew. When the *Rattler*'s river contingent got wind of the Confederate action, they fired their cannon at the church, lodging a cannonball in her front wall that remains imbedded there to this day.

The soldiers' violation of the Sabbath foreshadowed the disasters that would later befall the Rodney Church incident's participants. The *Rattler*'s string of bad luck continued until she was finally lost in the Mississippi off Grand Gulf during gale-force winds. Rodney fared no better, suffering wartime bombardment and several peacetime fires, ultimately meeting its end shortly after 1869 when the Mississippi River changed its course and consigned Rodney to oblivion. Of this drama's principals, only the Presbyterian Church endures, stately as the day she was built, a somber centerpiece of the river country's most famous ghost town—and, some might say, a perpetual reminder of the divine admonition to keep the Sabbath Day holy!

GIVING THEM THE FINGER

The Mississippi river country's most photographed structure is the Port Gibson Presbyterian Church, which sports a steeple consisting of a twelve-foot-tall gold hand and a six-foot-tall forefinger pointing dramatically toward heaven. The church was built in 1859 at a cost of $40,000 by Rev. Zebulon Butler, but the hand wasn't added until after his death. While ministering to his flock at another location during the 1850s, Butler zealously opposed slavery, often punctuating his sermons with an upraised hand and fully extended finger. He backed up his beliefs by helping 300 slaves return to Africa over strenuous local objection. But despite his antislavery views, Butler was so popular with his congregation that they retained him as their pastor throughout his career. And after Butler's funeral iron-ically proved to be the new church's first service, they erected a wooden hand in memory of his finger-raising sermons. Agnostic woodpeckers later convinced them to install a metal hand in the 1890s.

Presbyterian Church steeple, Port Gibson

The present Presbyterian Church contains an original gallery from which slaves worshiped on Sundays, and a chandelier taken from the famous steamboat *Robert E. Lee*. All would have been lost, though, but for the impression the original "hand" made upon General Grant. After winning the Battle of Port Gibson, Grant quartered at a home just across the street from the Presbyterian Church. In what must have been as much a tribute to the "church with the finger pointing upward" as to Port Gibson itself, Grant spared the village after his conquest, saying it was "too beautiful to destroy."

FALL OF THE HOUSE OF WINDSOR

One of the Mississippi river country's most impressive antebellum mansions was Port Gibson's elegant Windsor. Built in 1859-61 by wealthy planter S. C. Daniel, the house and furnishings cost $125,000 and $50,000, respectively, over and above the free carpentry and masonry supplied by 400 slaves. The epitome of Greek Revival style architecture, Windsor featured brick exterior walls, four floors, and an observatory and was surrounded by twenty-nine forty-five-foot-high columns joined by Italian wrought-iron railings. Double front doors graced the second and third stories, and a 145-foot-long veranda encircled the house on three sides.

Mississippi's largest antebellum mansion, Windsor stood sixty-five feet wide and sixty-four feet long. Its custom-made furniture, mostly rosewood and oak, came exclusively from Europe. Gold-framed mirrors and marble furnishings enhanced many of the thirty-two rooms. Persian rugs covered the floors, red velvet draperies and tapestry panels adorned the walls, and tremendous crystal chandeliers hung from ten- and sixteen-foot-high ceilings. Observing it from a riverboat, Mark Twain once opined that Windsor was too large to be a residence and must surely have been a local college.

The home was nearly burned by Grant's soldiers when a Union guard was shot in the front doorway, but the ole miss persuaded Grant that her family was innocent of the shooting. Windsor again almost met its end when Federals grew suspicious that flashing light messages were being sent to Louisiana from its balconies, but the lady of the house successfully hid the signal equipment from Yankee searchers.

Then, years after the war's end, on February 17, 1890, during a fateful house party, several partygoers ascended to the observatory to gain a better view of the Mississippi River. On his way back down, a young reveler tossed a cigarette into some trash left by carpenters effecting repairs. As guests gathered around a piano in a far room, a house servant shouted, "Fire!" Efforts to extinguish the blaze failed, and the mansion, twice saved from certain destruction during the war, met with a fiery peacetime death. All that remained were twenty-two Corinthian columns, which to this day continue to provide one of the Mississippi river country's greatest photo opportunities.

But even a fiery death failed to prevent Windsor from reappearing on history's stage (and screen). The ruins were first featured in the popular 1960s movie *Raintree County,*

Windsor ruins, Port Gibson

starring Elizabeth Taylor. Then, in 1990, while meeting with potential star witness Delmar Dennis in the midst of Windsor's ruins, Hinds County prosecutor Bobby DeLaughter convinced Dennis to testify against Byron De La Beckwith for the 1963 murder of civil-rights activist Medgar Evers. Beckwith's 1994 murder conviction finally avenged the death of one of the river country's greatest heroes and laid to rest one of Mississippi's most haunting ghosts. Then, in 1997, DeLaughter's and Dennis's historic meeting was reenacted before the cameras on Windsor's grounds for the filming of director Rob Reiner's *Ghosts of Mississippi.*

Along with grandeur and destruction, irony had finally come to Windsor. The ruins of this once magnificent plantation, built largely by slave labor, served as the backdrop for righting a terrible wrong against civil-rights leader Medgar Evers, his wife and children, and all law-abiding Mississippi river-country citizens.

ALMA MARTYR

Formed on the campus in 1860, a company of University of Mississippi students called the University Grays fought at Bull Run, Seven Pines, Frayser's Farm, Antietam, Gettysburg, the Wilderness, Spotsylvania, Cold Harbor, Petersburg, and finally

Appomattox. At Gettysburg, every boy in their unit was killed, wounded, or captured, but not before they achieved the high-water mark of the Confederacy by breaching the stone wall at Brian's Barn on Cemetary Ridge. According to historian David Sansing, a mortally wounded Gray, Jeremiah Gage, wrote his mother:

> This is the last you may ever hear from me. I have to tell you that I died like a man. . . . Remember that I am true to my country and my greatest regret at dying is that she is not free. . . . This letter is stained with my blood.

NO HARD FEELINGS

Despite the hardships they endured during the war, Mississippi river-country women put aside their antipathy and took a giant step towards binding up the nation's wounds in 1866. This event occurred in Columbus, Mississippi, in the heart of the Tombigbee River valley, where several women were paying their respects to several thousand Confederate dead in Odd Fellows Cemetery. There, they happened to notice that the graves of some forty Union soldiers had fallen into disrepair. The ladies appealed to their friends and neighbors, who joined them in grooming and decorating the Union graves. Other communities soon followed suit, and the press got wind of the whole affair and touted Columbus as the place where "flowers healed a nation." The ladies' Columbus Decoration Day eventually evolved into one of our nation's favorite holidays—Memorial Day!

Beauvoir, Jefferson Davis's final home, Biloxi

STAMPED OUT

Although the Mississippi river country never produced a president of the United States, it did give the Confederacy its one and only chief executive, Jefferson Davis. Davis was many things to many people—a traitor to Northerners, a symbol of the American South to Europeans, just another slave owner to African-Americans, a hero of the Lost Cause to many Southerners, an honorable gentleman to his congressional colleagues, and an unfairly imprisoned martyr to his friends, neighbors, and family. But to one ex-Confederate soldier who accosted him on the street some years after the war, Davis was something else entirely.

"Ain't you the president of the Confederate States?" asked the man, astonished to be suddenly in presence of greatness.

"I am, sir," Davis replied.

"Well, by God," said the former rebel soldier, "I *thought* you looked like a postage stamp!"

In his last public speech, Davis, formerly one of the most rabid of all secessionist fire-eaters, embraced the need for reconciliation, saying, "The past is dead; let it bury its dead, its hopes and aspirations. . . . Let me beseech you to lay aside all bitter sectional feelings, and to take your places in the ranks of those who will bring about a reunited country."

Chapter Six

GOT THOSE RECONSTRUCTION BLUES

The War Between the States lasted only four years, but the Reconstruction period that followed dragged on for another twelve years. Those trying years saw the bilking of honest Southerners by greedy Northern capitalists, enormous sacrifices by ex-slaves attempting to chart their own destinies, the refusal of white Southern leaders to help the former bondsmen achieve that goal, the rise of the Ku Klux Klan, and the United States government's ultimate failure to mollify wartime animosities and to accord the privilege of first-class citizenship to freedmen. But even this dark time produced rich examples of courage, integrity, and even humor in the face of oft-deadly political unrest. From L. Q. C. Lamar to Charles Caldwell, many river-country denizens strove mightily to bind up the nation's wounds and establish a government by and for all the nation's people.

Old Capitol Museum (1839), Jackson

GETTING THE CHAFF

Many antebellum river-country whites so loved their way of life they were willing to make untold sacrifices in support of the Confederacy's "Cause." Their slaves, on the other hand, felt very differently about the survival of the antebellum Southern way of life. Even under the best conditions, African bondsmen endured endless labors, personal degradation, and, worst of all, the impossibility of charting their own destinies. Not the least of their troubles were their meager diet, poor medical care, and wretched living quarters. A visitor once described north Mississippi plantation slave dwellings as "small, dilapidated and dingy; . . . there were no windows. There were spaces of several inches between the logs, through which there was clear vision. Everything within the cabins was colored by black smoke."

Despite these circumstances, slave owners originally viewed slavery as a "necessary evil," and by the 1860s defended the institution as "not a curse, but a blessing, as the legitimate condition of the African race."

And although several thousand freedmen and slaves voluntarily served alongside Confederates during the latter stages of the war, slavery was one of history's few institutions of which 100 percent of its members greeted its demise with unmitigated approval. An old slave song gives perfect expression to this sentiment and exposes the lie inherent in the antebellum argument that slavery benefited the slaves as well as their masters:

> *We raise de wheat; dey gib us de corn.*
> *We bake de bread; dey gib us de cruss.*
> *We sif' de meal; dey gib us de huss.*
> *We peel de meat; dey gib us de skin.*
> *And dat's de way dey takes us in.*

The end of the Civil War brought hope to the former bondsmen, but they soon discovered that the new government's promise of "forty acres and mule" for every hardworking freedman was made with the same forked tongue that had promised river-country Indians that they could trust Uncle Sam's support when push came to shove.

FROG-POND POLITICS

As Mr. Faulkner once said, "the past is never dead; it's never even past," and the horrors inflicted by American slavery, the Civil War, and Reconstruction violence left gaping wounds in the national consciousness that may survive well into the twenty-first century. Republican Reconstruction, which had its genesis in the now-familiar strains of Southern recalcitrance and Northern hypocrisy, brought even greater postwar suffering to Southern whites, false hopes of freedom to African-Americans, and unprecedented anger towards enterprising Northern "carpetbaggers." Attempting to enforce assassinated President Lincoln's plan of reconciliation, Andrew Johnson battled vengeful Radical Republicans on one hand and Southern white supremacists on the other. Johnson pleaded with the latter to grant enfranchisement to "all persons of color who can read the Constitution in English and write their names, and to [blacks] who own real estate valued at not less than two hundred and fifty dollars, and pay taxes thereon."

By so doing, the compromise-oriented Johnson reasoned, Mississippi officials would place the South on the same basis as the Northern states insofar as the new freedmen were concerned, thereby nullifying Northern radicals' complaints about continued Southern resistance. Of course, Johnson's words fell on deaf ears in Mississippi, where the legislature passed a Black Code that, under the guise of requiring blacks to work, practically reestablished the hardships of Southern slavery. The Northern press issued a scathing response, saying, "We tell the white men of Mississippi that the men of the North will convert [the state] into a frog pond before they will allow any such laws to disgrace one foot of soil in which the bones of our soldiers sleep and over which the flag of freedom flies."

More significantly, Congress impeached Johnson and passed several Reconstruction Acts, which initiated the Radical Republicans' much harsher postwar measures. And even though the North conducted Reconstruction in a reasonably fair manner to both Southern whites and blacks, whites resisted every measure to the best of their abilities, and the new freedmen soon discovered that Northern politicians were no more interested in guaranteeing the South's ex-slaves' continued freedom than they were in granting Northern blacks all of their basic human rights. When African-American Mississippi congressman Blanche K. Bruce resigned his post in 1881, he opined that he would be the last black to serve in the U.S. Senate. His words proved prophetic, as the U.S. Senate remained segregated for another eighty-five years until Massachusetts elected an African-American senator in 1966.

CAME, SAW, CONQUERED

For blacks on the front line of Reconstruction efforts, life was a constant struggle and, if the most violent would-be Redeemers had anything to do with it, tragically short. So it was with Clinton blacksmith Charles Caldwell, who was born a slave and later served as one of sixteen black Republican delegates to Mississippi's 1868 Constitutional Convention. Shortly thereafter he became the first black man to shoot and kill a white assailant, go to trial, and get acquitted by an all-white jury. He was elected as Hinds County's state senator in 1870 and also served as leader of the state militia during the Revolt of 1875, an association that later cost him his life.

On September 4, 1875, Democrat "White Liners" revolted against the Republican state government, shooting or lynching fifty black and white Republican leaders in Clinton. Caldwell escaped, but the armed men assured his wife that they would kill him "if it is two years, or one year, or six." Then, when President Grant refused Gov. Adelbert Ames' request for federal troops, Ames called out the state militia, placing Caldwell in charge of Company A, Second Regiment, Mississippi Infantry. On October 9, Captain Caldwell and his 102 black soldiers marched from Jackson to Edwards then back to Clinton, picking up an additional 100 black militia on the way. Faced with this determined army of freedmen, the

White Liners backed down, and further violence was averted. Of his actions during the insurrection, the Jackson Weekly Pilot said, "If Capt. Caldwell ever talks Latin he can say veni, vidi, vici, which means: I carried the guns to Edwards Depot and have returned with twice as many men as I started with. What an excellent recruiting officer the Captain would make."

However, on Christmas Day 1875, vengeful whites carried out their death threats against Caldwell. After accepting an invitation for a drink from several Clinton businessmen, Caldwell was shot in the back as they all raised their glasses in a toast. Although the White Liners finally succeeded in silencing Caldwell, his dying words to members of the back-shooting mob etched a permanent mark in the history of river-country courage:

> Remember when you kill me, you kill a gentleman and a brave man. Never say you killed a coward. I want you to remember it when I'm gone.

CONSTITUTIONAL QUIBBLES

After the war, the Radical Republicans forced new state constitutions upon the rebellious Southern state legislatures. In Mississippi, the Constitution of 1869 was so detested by whites that its provisions had to be enforced by federal troops. This met with much criticism from the local press, including the following editorial from one Clarion-Ledger pundit, who opined that the '69 Constitution's preamble should have read:

> We, the aliens, strangers, carpetbaggers, and ignoramuses, assembled in Convention by the grace of [Republican governor] Adelbert Ames, are highly gratified that we have the power to force upon the people of Mississippi, at the power of the bayonet, the following Constitution, and to give them just such a government as we desire that they shall have.

After the white Democrats regained power, a new Constitutional Convention was convened in 1890. Two hotly contested issues at the convention were whether the freedmen were to be enfranchised and whether they should be allowed a decent public education. Many planter-statesmen supported both measures, with L. Q. C. Lamar publicly declaring that he would "leave no legitimate effort unused and no constitutional means unemployed" to grant black citizens their right to an education. Nevertheless, the majority succeeded in defeating all efforts to provide a separate-but-equal black public-school system, and in writing an "Understanding Clause" into the 1890 Constitution. This provision denied the vote to those, especially ex-slaves with no education, who could not read and interpret clauses of the U.S. Constitution.

Objecting to this document, another Clarion-Ledger columnist offered $100 to anyone who could "understand the new Constitution," and added:

> The [Constitution] has proven a "mess" from first to last. Nobody understands it. The plain people do not comprehend it; the lawyers cannot interpret it . . . and the Supreme Court judges cannot fathom its mysteries. . . . Talk about "understanding clause," there seems to be no clause in the instrument that anybody understands.

Governor's Mansion (1842), Jackson

But despite any and all objections, the 1890 Constitution showed great staying power and, with various amendments, including a twentieth-century repeal of the "Understanding Clause," remains in force in Mississippi today.

BEND; DON'T BREAK

Isaiah T. Montgomery, a former Warren County slave, had the most unusual career of any prominent Reconstruction Era official. While serving as a cabin boy in the Union navy during the battles of Grand Gulf and Vicksburg, Montgomery watched General Grant institute the Davis Bend experiment, designed to establish a colony of self-sufficient ex-slaves on the Mississippi River. Located thirty miles south of Vicksburg on land formerly owned by Jefferson Davis and his brother Joseph, Davis Bend soon seemed every bit the "Negro Paradise" Grant intended when he arranged for 70 black men to purchase 30 acres apiece. The freedmen swiftly transformed 5,000 acres into a thriving community of 1,800 blacks, several general stores, a school and school board, free medical services, and a sheriff and judge for 181 separate districts. In 1866, Montgomery purchased the Davises' plantations and tripled his investment his first year.

But when the Davises successfully sued for the return of all their property in 1878, Montgomery led Davis Bend settlers upriver to the Delta, where they founded the South's first all-black town, Mound Bayou. In 1879, Montgomery traveled to Wyandotte, Kansas, where he established a farm community for the Black Exodusters, a group of freedmen fleeing the South. When Teddy Roosevelt sought an honest man to serve as Mississippi's receiver of public moneys in 1892, he chose Montgomery to handle that weighty responsibility.

Accepting the position during the cornerstone-laying ceremony for the Lincoln Memorial in Washington, D.C., Montgomery spoke as one of the four million slaves who received the priceless boon of liberty "through the stroke of [Lincoln's] pen, and as a representative of ten million Negro citizens of our beloved country." Lincoln had been, Montgomery proclaimed, a man of "exceeding humble birth, rocked in the cradle of adversity, but chosen of God [as] the prophet of human liberty and the liberator of not merely four million black men, but of the minds and hearts of his countrymen."

Montgomery's political career reached a controversial peak during Mississippi's 1890 Constitutional Convention, when, as the sole black delegate to the convention, he supported voting restrictions for blacks that kept them out of Mississippi politics for over seventy more years. In an hour-long convention address, Montgomery declared, "I am willing that the Negro be disenfranchised because he is ignorant, but I am not willing that he should be disenfranchised because he is black. And if intelligence is to be made the test of suffrage, I insist that the white man shall submit to the same requirements imposed on the black man." He finished by admitting that by supporting the controversial "Understanding Clause" provisions, he was making a "fearful sacrifice laid upon the burning altar of liberty," but did so to ensure peaceful relations between the races by temporarily keeping blacks out of the emotionally charged political process.

Montgomery was later elected mayor of Mound Bayou, and when Montgomery established an oil mill and manufacturing company for the town in 1912, Booker T. Washington labeled his business the greatest commercial and manufacturing enterprise in the history of the black race. After Isaiah Montgomery died in 1924, ten local white planters chipped in to pay for his tombstone, which, along with the town he founded, continues to serve as a memorial to Mound Bayou's enigmatic founder.

HIRAM SEZ: HIRE 'EM

Although Reconstruction only brought temporary relief to river-country blacks, one of their greatest leaders brought them hope during the best and worst of those times. This was the United States' first black U.S. congressman, a Natchez minister named Hiram Rhoades Revels. Ordained as a pastor of the African Methodist Episcopal Church in Philadelphia, Pennsylvania, Revels recruited blacks for the Union army in St. Louis and Baltimore during the early stages of the war. In 1864 he came to Vicksburg to establish schools for freedmen, and subsequently moved to Natchez to pastor the Bethel A.M.E. Church. In

1870, the Republican Reconstruction government elected him state senator from Adams County, and later that year, Revels was appointed by Mississippi governor Alcorn to fill Jefferson Davis's empty U.S. Senate seat.

Although the Northern press falsely accused Revels of being unqualified and of engaging in immoral conduct, a Southern newspaper, the Mobile Register, defended Revels, declaring that "if immorality were made the test, the Senate would be swept clean of its members." After three days of hearings over his credentials, during which all charges were fully answered and dropped, Revels officially took office on February 24, 1870. Dressed in his clerical black suit and long coat, carrying black gloves and a brown cane, Revels became the United States' first black senator.

Ever the conservative reconciliator, Revels suffered harsh criticism from the Radicals for supporting the readmission of Georgia to the Union. Declaring that Georgia freedmen bore "toward their former masters no revengeful thoughts, no hatreds, no animosities," Revels protested "in the name of truth and human rights against any and every attempt to fetter the hands of 100,000 white and colored citizens in the state of Georgia." He also magnanimously advocated amnesty for all former Mississippi Confederates willing to pledge loyalty to the Union.

In 1871 he advocated integration of Washington, D.C. schools, appointed an African-American to West Point, and got blacks hired as mechanics in the U.S. Navy yards. In May

New Capitol Building (1903), Jackson

of that year, Revels and Governor Alcorn prepared a bill to provide for what would later become Mississippi's first black university. Instituted with a budget of $50,000, the same as that of the University of Mississippi's, Alcorn A & M College (later Alcorn State University) opened its doors, with Revels serving as its first president. Although the Mississippi legislature expressed a desire to name the college after Revels, he modestly suggested that it bear Governor Alcorn's name.

The black pastor who replaced the Confederacy's president in the U.S. Senate served his church, college, and country well, and three-quarters of a century would pass before Mississippi state politics would again experience the preeminence of admirable public servants such as L. Q. C. Lamar, Blanche K. Bruce, and Hiram Rhoades Revels.

Chapter Seven

MISSISSIPPI MYTHCONCEPTIONS

While the Mississippi river country ranks second to none as a stage for extraordinary characters and historic dramas, it also rates as an excellent source of Native, Anglo-, and African-American legend. The folk inhabiting our region have always loved a good story, and that estimable quality has produced everything from America's greatest Indian orators to many of the nation's best-loved novelists. It has also led to the proliferation of mythic tales from every corner of the river-country melting pot, stories that are in no way diminished by their tenuous connection to reality.

Haunted antebellum mansion, Stanton Hall, Natchez

MYTHING PERSONS

The Pascagoula River, which flows into the Gulf of Mexico near present-day Pascagoula, is locally known as the "Singing River" for a mysterious melody emanating from its waters. In 1699, Iberville noted the peculiar noise, and in 1727, Governor Perier described the sound as a "distant concert of a thousand Eolian harps." Modern-day visitors liken it to a "swarm of bees in flight," best heard during the quiet of a midsummer's evening. This sound has been attributed to numerous as yet unproven causes, such as an unknown species of fish, the movement of sand across the river's bottom, currents sucked past a hidden cave, mosquito swarms, and natural gas escaping nearby sand beds. Legend, too, is in disagreement regarding the music's source. Four stories offer differing explanations for the riddle of the Singing River, although each of them features a now vanished local Indian tribe.

In 1850, Charles Gayarre published the version first told to the French a century and a half earlier. On the Pascagoula's banks, near the place where the "music" may now be heard, lived an ancient Indian tribe called the Pascagoula. This tribe was very different

The legendary Singing River, Moss Point and Pascagoula

from the others in the region, who believed the Pascagoula to be former ocean dwellers. The Pascagoula were distinguished by their unusually light complexions, their propensity for indolence, their peculiar diet of oysters and fish, and their love of festivals. Most of their carnivals centered around their mermaid goddess, whose statue they worshiped with "soul-stirring" music. Then, in 1539, one of De Soto's men, a priest even lighter complected than they, appeared on their river's banks. Speaking to the Indians in their own language, the priest immediately set about the task of converting them to Christianity.

Just as the priest began making converts, the mermaid deity appeared over the river's waters at midnight on the evening of a full moon, and in an enchanting voice, sang, "Come to me, come to me, children of the sea; neither bell, book, nor cross shall win ye from your queen." Bewitched by her song, the entire tribe plunged into the river and drowned. The priest died from grief, believing that he had failed to save the Pascagoula from the powers of darkness. The nearby tribes later informed the French that the music's source was the sound of their lost Pascagoula brethren, singing their mermaid's praises at the bottom of the river.

The second legend is more romantic than religious. Olustee, the son of the Pascagoula's chief, fell in love with Miona, a maiden of the nearby Biloxi tribe. Although she was betrothed to Otanga, the chief of the warlike Biloxi, Miona ultimately agree to come live with Olustee and his people. On the eve of their wedding, Otanga led a Biloxi raid against the sleeping Pascagoula. Olustee begged the Pascagoula to turn him over to the Biloxi, but they refused. Knowing their cause to be hopeless, the Pascagoula committed mass suicide rather than suffer enslavement. They gathered at the river, where the braves, chanting their death song, led the whole tribe into the murky depths. Miona and Olustee were the last to disappear beneath the waves, and their mournful song is heard even to this day.

Another tale of star-crossed lovers is the subject of the third Singing River legend. A Pascagoula chief's joy over the birth of his son was cut short when the child and one of the chief's wives disappeared the next night. The tribe searched for a baby boy with a birthmark on his thigh resembling a bunch of unripe berries, but their search proved fruitless. Years later, the chief's second wife gave him a daughter named Kai-ce. Sometime after Kai-ce reached womanhood, a stranger came to the Pascagoula, a young man who brought a stirring message of peace to the tribe. After a swift rise to prominence, the young man fell in love with Kai-ce. Although the uncertainty of his parentage was at first an obstacle to their betrothal, the young brave's persistence finally paid off and the two lovers were happily wed. The morning after the ceremony, the young bride told her mother about a strange birthmark on her new husband's thigh. Her mother's inspection revealed the tragic truth that Kai-ce's husband was also her long-lost brother. With their marriage declared unlawful, the young brave gave his bride a final embrace, chanted, "Hip-co-toggony-huni-bug-ee-cha," and leaped to his death in the river. Still heard to this day is Kai-ce's mournful song, sung as she wasted away on the river's banks after her beloved's watery demise.

The fourth legend is yet another French and Indian tale of ill-fated romance. In 1734, Perique Quave and eighty French and Canadian families came to reside by the Pascagoula

River, establishing a settlement in an area between the Pascagoula and Mohocti tribes. The whites enjoyed friendly relations with both tribes and settled into a paradise of daily festivals, abundant fish and game, and the most beautiful flora they had ever seen. During one especially lovely sunset on the riverbank, two lovers, Perique's son, Bullo, and the daughter of Mohocti chief Kobiana, heard a beguiling song. It went:

> Land of love and song and dance, land of islands, sweet romance,
> Land of palms and singing streams, land of music and of dreams,
> Summer spends the winter here, birds and flowers all the year.
> To this land of dreams come true the river's calling you.

Amid the great oaks and Spanish moss, the lovers found Pascagoula princess Anola, La Glorieuse, singing in concert with the melodious river. "I am teaching the river to sing," she told the astonished lovers.

Some days later, Bullo and a Pascagoula hunting party found a man nearly dead of hunger and exposure. He was Cosauk, the son of the chief of the Biloxi tribe twenty miles to the west. Knowing that the warlike Biloxi would kill any Pascagoula who brought them bad news, but would not take such punitive measures with anyone else, Pascagoula chief Altama sent Bullo to the Biloxi to tell them what had become of Cosauk. Unaware of the bad blood between the two tribes, and seeking only to allay a worried father's fears, Bullo concocted a story for the Biloxi chief that Cosauk had fallen in love with Princess Anola and would soon return to his people with a new bride on his arm. Enraged at this turn of events, the Biloxi chief decided to attack the Pascagoula.

Bullo returned with the bad news, only to discover that a fever had wiped out all but twenty Pascagoula families. He took the still very ill Cosauk to the Mohocti village, where the chief selected his own daughter to nurse the fallen Biloxi back to health. Needless to say, Cosauk and the maiden fell deeply in love. When the Biloxi arrived ready for battle a few days later, Bullo and Chief Kobiana invited them to an evening of feast and dance courtesy of the Mohocti. The festival lasted all night, and the Biloxi were so tired the next day they had to delay their attack upon the Pascagoula another twenty-four hours.

During that one day's reprieve, the Pascagoula contrived a plan to avoid bloodshed. When the Biloxi arrived on the river's banks the next day, they found a village populated only with a few old men and some women. Princess Anola told them that, rather than suffer certain defeat at the mighty Biloxi's hands, her tribesmen had marched into the river singing their death chants, preferring a watery death to life as Biloxi slaves. In the silence that followed, the Biloxi warriors heard the river singing the song that Anola had taught it. The awestruck Biloxi returned to their village, and the Pascagoula and Mohocti resumed their peaceful coexistence, perpetually serenaded by the Anola-trained Singing River.

A POSSUM'S TALE AND A DOG'S LIFE

The Biloxi told the French many stories that explained how the animals developed their present-day characteristics. According to one of their legends, the Ancient of Opossums killed a wolf, then walked around with a wolf's-teeth necklace dangling around his neck, proudly singing about his bold deed. When asked by the Ancient of Wolves why he sang, the Ancient of Opossums lied and said he was singing about the area's pretty flowers. Later, the wolves discovered the deception and resolved to punish the killer. Just as they were about to execute him, the Ancient of Opossums told them that if they hit him with a stick he would not die, but that if they fashioned a stick from a dead tree with the bark peeled off and struck him with that, he would surely die. As they searched for the deadly stick, the Opossum made good his escape through a hole in the ground. Several times the Opossum reemerged from the ground, each time tricking the wolves into believing he was someone else by virtue of a painted-on disguise. Finally, while underground and believing himself to be beyond their reach, he confessed his identity to the wolves. But unbeknownst to him, his bushy tail protruded from the hole and the wolves seized it and stripped off the fur. Since that day, possums' tails have been little more than skin and bone.

Another Biloxi legend told how the Wild Turkey killed many humans, took their scalps, and wore human-hair necklaces. This, they said, gave rise to the modern-day turkey's tuft of hair. He also strung human fingernails around his legs, thereby creating the present-day ridges above turkeys' feet. Unable to catch the speedy Wild Turkey, the humans sent their friend the Dog to kill him. After the Dog succeeded in dispatching with the troublesome bird, the humans feted him with a dinner of the best victuals available. Instead of eating the delicious entrees, the Dog declared, "I am going to eat the food that others leave," and gobbled up a bowl of mush. That is why dogs eat leftovers.

These and other similar legends may also explain why everyone studied Aesop's Fables in school, and not the Biloxi's charming, but mostly pointless, tales.

THE GREAT SPIRIT IN THE GARDEN OF EDEN

The Biloxi Indian version of the Garden of Eden is very similar to the biblical account, although its postscript adds a new dimension to the story. After creating an Indian as the first man, the Great One Above, Kuti Mankdce, created a second person, an Indian maiden, while the man slept. The god then went in search of food for his new creations. But when the humans awoke, the evil being named Another Person said to them, "Why have you not eaten of the fruit of this tree? I think He has made it for you two to eat." The woman promptly stewed the fruit of the tree and she and the man dined heartily. When Kuti Mankdce returned, he grew angry at their actions and said, "Work for yourself and find food, because you shall be hungry."

Sometime later, their god sent them a letter, but the Indians did not receive it. The Americans got it and it was they who first learned how to read and write. After the letter incident, the Americans found a stream of water and washed themselves in it. Next the Frenchmen came to bathe, then the Indians. Because the river became muddier every time any group used it, the first bathers were lighter complected than subsequent bathers. By the time the Spanish came around, the river was quite muddy. But when the Africans finally arrived, they received the darkest color of all. After bathing, the Africans washed off their palms, the only place where they are not darker than the others.

PUBLIC-OPINION POLES

An ancient Choctaw legend accounts for both the Choctaws' and the Chickasaws' origins. In the distant past, from an opening in a sacred mound called Nanih Waiya, strode the full-grown Cherokee and Chickasaw. When the mound opened a second time, the Choctaw came forth from Mother Earth.

A less fanciful tale, jointly held by many Choctaws and Chickasaws, not only provides their river-country origins but also helps explain the many similarities in their language, customs, and characteristics. As the story goes, the tribes were formerly one Muskhogean-speaking nation residing in the far west "where the Sun disappears." Two brothers, Chacta and Chicksa, led their people east by placing a sacred pole in the ground each evening, and moving in the direction it leaned the next morning. After crossing the Mississippi River, they camped in present-day Winston County along the Noxubee River's banks. The next morning, Chacta discovered the sacred pole standing upright, and it was there that he and many of his people, later known as the Choctaws, remained. However, the brothers had a falling out, and Chicksa led a contingent across the river and started a separate tribe, which would later become known as the Chickasaws.

Three aspects of this second legend give it more credence than most Choctaw/Chickasaw origin stories. First, these two Mississippi tribes had so much in common that the tale may be more fact than fiction. Second, throughout the course of river-country history, the warlike Chickasaws never got along with the more peacefully inclined Choctaws, so this original spat comes as no great surprise. Finally, considering the numerous documented squabbles that took place on its banks, the Noxubee River was a prime source of contention and may well have served as the original site of controversy between the Muskhogean peoples.

MOUND OF BABBLE

After considering the teachings of early missionaries, the Choctaws developed yet another theory of how there came to be so many different-speaking river-country tribes. According to this legend, Aba, the Great Spirit, originally fashioned many men out of the earth's yellow clay, all of whom spoke the language of the Choctaw. Mesmerized by the clouds and blue sky above them, the men built a giant mound out of stones so they could reach up and touch the sky. But after night fell, a great wind blew and the men and their stones came tumbling to the ground. When they awoke the next morning, they found themselves unharmed but unable to understand each other's words. Some continued to speak the old language, and from these came the Choctaw tribe. Unable to understand each other, the

Emerald Mound, near Natchez

rest began fighting amongst themselves. These ultimately went their separate ways, forming all the other tribes throughout the world.

DAVY CROCKETT OF THE PEARL

Pearl River County, situated southwest of Hattiesburg and northeast of Gulfport, is, along with several other counties, home to the river from which it took its name. It is also where trapper John Spiers garnered legendary status as the Davy Crockett of the Pearl River. According to the legend, Spiers not only cleared the area of wolves, he also killed hundreds of bears, one while he was armed with only a pocketknife.

Spiers had found a lonely bear cub and was carrying it through a thickly wooded area when the cub's mother suddenly appeared out of the underbrush with teeth bared and claws primed for action. Without time to run or hide, Spiers dropped the cub, drew his pocketknife, and charged the enraged mama bear. When they collided, the bear's right paw ripped the flesh from Spiers' shoulder as her great maw reached for his throat. But Spiers' knife punctured the bear's heart and she died before breaking his neck with her massive jaws. Spiers stumbled home with a torn shoulder and bleeding throat, and, despite the lack of medical attention, fully recovered from his wounds. He later resumed a long and eventful career as the Pearl River's most celebrated bear hunter. The legend is silent as to whether Spiers remained in Pearl River County in the 1860s or caught the martial fever that took the real Davy Crockett's life thirty years earlier.

THE ULTIMATE DISGRACE

Federal troops vandalized central Mississippi's Jasper County during the Civil War, stealing cattle, looting houses, and burning barns along the Tallahala River. These acts naturally led to a long-standing hatred of Yankees by that region's citizens. To this day they tell the story of a young lady who fell in love with and married a Northerner during an eastern sojourn and brought him home to meet her Jasper County relatives. As the story goes, a little grandson grew anxious when the family skirted the usual rooms and convened in the parlor, which was ordinarily reserved for funerals and weddings. When the concerned young boy asked his mother if anyone had died, she replied, "No one is dead, but something worse has happened. Your aunt Sue has gone and married a Yankee!"

GHOSTS OF MISSISSIPPI

The ghosts of the Mississippi river country are plentiful, and they've manifested themselves in every century and in every conceivable form and locale. The phantoms of sixteenth-century Spanish soldiers often appear in the fog arising from Natchez's Mississippi River bluffs, while the shades of eighteenth-century French soldiers still frequent the area near old Fort Rosalie, where the Natchez Indians massacred them in 1729. The ghosts of early-nineteenth-century land pirates Wiley Harpe, Sam Mason, and John Murrell often accost nighttime Trace travelers, and bandit Joseph Thompson Hare was himself once terrified by an early 1800s encounter with a white, spectral stallion. The ghost of a child Harpe murdered, along with several other notorious spooks, still haunts Natchez's King's Tavern Restaurant. And every Halloween an unknown phantom rides a stagecoach along the upper Trace just north of French Camp and only thirty-five miles from where Greenwood LeFlore's great mansion, Malmaison, once stood.

There's also a river-country ghost ship, the side-wheeler *Eliza Battle,* which appears on stormy nights on the Tombigbee River between Columbus and Mobile. It was on that river that she sank in 1858 because of an unexpected winter snowstorm. Witnesses often report seeing the ghost ship's cotton bales ablaze, and hearing both the calliope's happy tunes and the sixty lost passengers' bloodcurdling screams.

There's even the Witch of Yazoo City, who, according to noted Yazoo author Willie Morris, died in quicksand after a sordid career of luring local fishermen to their deaths. According to the legend, before she died, the old hag threatened to break out of her grave and burn down Yazoo City. And despite the townspeople's precaution of placing a heavy chain over her grave, Yazoo City suffered a terrible fire in 1904. Subsequent inspection of the witch's grave revealed that the chain had been inexplicably broken in two.

But perhaps the most intriguing of these river-country spirits are the ones inhabiting those prominent reminders of the South's haunted past—her antebellum mansions. Although popular during pilgrimage season for their extraordinary architecture and extravagant furnishings, these mansions are also renowned for the ghosts that inhabit them. A classic example is that of Natchez's Dunleith.

Reminiscent of an ancient Greek temple, Dunleith mansion is surrounded by two-story Tuscan columns and scroll-like brackets underneath the eaves. Typical of antebellum Greek Revival architecture, the house features double parlors separated by sliding doors, marble mantels, and floor-length windows opening onto spacious galleries, themselves beautifully outlined with cast-iron grillwork. But for all her majesty, no aspect of Dunleith surpasses the fame of her harp-playing ghost, Miss Percy.

Having fallen in love with a visiting Frenchman during the early 1800s, the ill-fated Miss Percy risked scandalous gossip to follow her lover to France in hope of inducing him to make good his promise of marriage. After the romance quickly soured, Miss Percy returned home to a tarnished reputation and moved into Dunleith with Mrs. Dahlgren, her relative by marriage. Thereafter, Miss Percy rarely ventured outside of Dunleith, passing her time playing her harp, until she died of a broken heart. A few days later, Mrs. Dahlgren heard the strange sound of harp music flowing from the parlor, only to hear the music end as she entered the room. To this day, harp music still reverberates off the walls of stately Dunleith.

Natchez's most palatial mansion, Stanton Hall, was built in the 1850s by an Irishman named Frederick Stanton, whose daughters' spirits remain in residence to this day. Another classic example of Greek Revival style, Stanton Hall is a two-story, three-room-deep brick structure adorned by fluted columns with Corinthian capitals, a gigantic triangular pediment with projecting scrolls, ornate rose-patterned iron grillwork, a two-and-one-half-inch-thick mahogany door fitted with silver doorknobs and hinges, and a looping staircase that rises to a cupola above. It was in a second-floor bedroom with appropriately black marble mantels that Stanton's two young daughters were murdered by Union soldiers for the silver service they had hidden under their bed. Their spirits continue to haunt the room years after their tragic wartime murders.

Natchez's most unique mansion, Longwood, was never completed because, in 1860, its Northern workers laid down their tools and left for Philadelphia at the outbreak of the Civil War. But the eerie scaffolding and paint buckets still cluttering Longwood's floors haven't prevented two ghosts from taking up residence within her walls. The largest octagonal house in America, Longwood sports a rotunda that opens to two floors, an attic, observatory, and crowning Oriental dome and spire. The other rooms open onto balconies embellished with Moorish arches or onto verandas decorated with foliated drapery. Apart from the exterior facade, the only functional part of the mansion is the basement, where the current owners reside. There, they have encountered the ghost of the home's builder, Dr. Haller Nutt, seated in a rocking chair, dressed in a ruffled white shirt and fitted pants. They've also seen the spirit of Nutt's wife, Julia, standing in a doorway accoutered in a hoop-skirt dress. These good folk may be forced to endure the ghosts of "Nutt's Folly" until they hire some more dependable Southern workmen who'll finish what the good doctor Nutt started in the nineteenth century.

Y'ALL COME BACK, Y'HEAR

Vicksburg is also home to numerous mansion-squatting ghosts, but that doesn't bother those homes' exceptionally unflappable river-city owners, who are simply delighted about having guests to entertain. One of these haunted mansions is Lakemont, a fine old Greek Revival home with an enormous front porch, French windows, and fluted porch columns with Ionic capitals. Back in the days of *Code Duelo,* Lakemont's mistress, Mrs. Lake, spilled a bottle of floral-scented perfume when informed that her husband, Judge William Lake, was preparing to fight a duel across the river in Louisiana. From her home's upstairs gallery, Mrs. Lake peered nervously through opera glasses at her husband's sandbar duel and, to her horror, saw him gunned down before her very eyes. Later residents have encountered Mrs. Lake walking on the porch or strolling in the garden and noticed the scent of jasminelike perfume in the air. But the new owners, in the fine tradition of Southern hospitality, don't begrudge Mrs. Lake her joint tenancy in their home. "She was here before we were," said John Wayne Jabour, "and seems to love this house like we do. She's just part of the family."

Bluff City haunted house Anchuca was originally built in Port Gibson in 1837 by wealthy planter Richard Archer but was later moved to Vicksburg. Another Greek Revival example, the two-and-a-half-story structure has two-story columns, fresco-decorated ceilings, wide halls, spacious rooms, and a brick dependency that houses a kitchen behind the residence. Archer sired five daughters, but was especially fond of the one who resembled him so closely that everyone called her "Archie." When Archie fell in love with the overseer's son, Archer sent the boy away to prevent her from marrying beneath her social station. The enraged Archie vowed never to take another meal with her family, and thereafter dined alone, standing beside the fireplace, using the marble mantel for a table. In 1966, the new owners, the Lavenders, dismantled Anchucha and rebuilt it in Vicksburg. Since that time, family members have reported sightings of a pretty eighteen-year-old girl in a brown dress standing by the mantel, undoubtedly still pining away for her socially unacceptable, long-lost love.

Two other famous Vicksburg Greek Revival style houses, Cedar Grove and Duff Green Mansion, are also haunted, the former being home to crying infant spirits and the latter often visited by a peg-legged Confederate soldier. However, Vicksburg's most extraordinary haunted house may be McRaven, which features three distinct architectural styles. The rear wing of McRaven was fashioned in 1797 in the Frontier style, i.e., two one-room-wide stories and a gallery, while another section was added in Empire or Creole style in 1836. These were followed in 1849 by an addition of the current front section done in the Greek Revival style with the familiar flying-wing stairway, marble mantels, and heavy millwork. Union soldiers shot and killed the 1860s owner in his garden, and he is presumed to be one of McRaven's supernatural residents. The current owner reports hearing ghostly footsteps and seeing lights turn on and off and piano stools move around by themselves. When recently asked if he minded being alone in McRaven, this intrepid soul calmly replied, "Who's alone?"

But the Mississippi River is not the only Magnolia State waterway with haunted houses on its banks. Fifteen miles east of West Point near the Tombigbee River sits the nineteenth-century, 50,000-acre Waverly Plantation. Two curved, freestanding staircases that rise from the downstairs ballroom to balconies on the second, third, and fourth floors highlight Waverly's opulence, as does a crowning sixteen-windowed cupola. The parlor, library, and dining room all measure twenty-two by twenty-five feet and sport unique features such as a wedding alcove, a built-in walnut secretary, and a built-in china cabinet, respectively. The millwork was of both Greek Revival and Egyptian style, and the outdoor opulence included formal gardens, orchards, a brick kiln, an icehouse, and a brick and marble swimming pool.

After the last Waverly passed away, the house fell into disrepair, but was restored in 1962 by Robert and Donna Snow. Two years after clearing away the cobwebs and bat's nests, the Snows discovered that their new home had also come with a built-in spook. The Snows began hearing a three-year-old girl's voice crying, "Mama, Mama," in an upstairs bedroom. Sometime later, Mrs. Snow discovered "an indention . . . on the bedspread, just as if a young child were sleeping on the bed in the afternoon, and it would be gone at night." One afternoon, the Snows watched spellbound as the indention and other bed-sheet wrinkles straightened themselves out as the ghost child arose from her slumber. The ghost's identity is still unknown, and she became visible only once, dressed in a nightgown on the stairway.

Errollton, a Greek Revival mansion fronted with Tudor arches, red-glassed transom lights, wooden tracery spandrels, and six octagonal columns, is another Tombigbee River haunted house. Built in 1848 by William Weaver, this Columbus mansion was home to "Miss Nellie," Weaver's daughter who, according to an 1878 tradition, used a diamond ring to etch her name on a windowpane the day of her engagement. After Douglas and Chebie Bateman purchased the home in 1950 and replaced all the windowpanes, the name *Nellie* mysteriously reappeared, scrawled in exactly the same hand as the original, on the same place on the new pane. Fortunately, Bateman had known and liked Miss Nellie before she died, and he and his wife welcomed her presence from the start. "I always felt," said Mrs. Bateman, "that she came back to tell us she was glad the house was occupied and that children's voices again filled the house."

These stories are nothing if not a tribute to river-country hospitality. Where other Americans run screaming out into the snow at the first hint of otherworldly guests,

Southerners invite their ghosts into the parlor to give piano recitals and enjoy late-night toddies, eventually sending them on their way with the familiar refrain, "Y'all come back, y'hear!"

WHO Y'ALL GONNA CALL?

One of the most spirit-inundated houses in Mississippi lies nestled in the heart of Tallahatchie River country in a quiet little hamlet called Holly Springs. It is Featherstone Place, built in 1834 by Tennessee merchant Alexander McEwen, who later named his adopted town after the holly trees abundant in the area. This lovely white, two-story clapboard structure is considered an example of Planter or English raised-basement-type architecture, with parlors and bedrooms on the first floor and dining rooms and a kitchen in the basement. Featherstone Place's claim to supernatural fame lies in the fact that it houses not one but three spectral residents.

One of its spirits often awakened a former Featherstone mistress by treading loudly up the stairs in large, heavy shoes. After the lady carpeted the stairway, that ghost was never heard from again. A second ghost, this one a beautiful, young woman, was often seen by other residents as it traversed the first-floor hallway. A third is an elderly woman dressed in dark clothing, a shawl, and a large cameo brooch, first seen standing over a horrified guest's baby's crib. She is believed to be Mrs. McEwen, who, while living out her golden years in Featherstone Place with her daughter and son-in-law, Gen. Winfield Scott Featherstone, informed them and everyone who would listen that she would stay in her house forever, always wearing her cameo brooch.

When recent owners Charlie and Jane Farris purchased Featherstone Place in 1998, they did so unaware of its haunted past. When they were later informed by Mississippi ghost-chasing author Katheryn Tucker Windham of their home's substantial ghost infestation, the Farrises' twelve-year-old daughter, Frannie, asked somewhat disconcertedly, "What?! Ghosts in our house?"

Perhaps Frannie and her younger brother, Buddy, should have resorted to Southern folklore remedies to banish Featherstone Place's ghosts from their new abode. These remedies include painting windows blue, planting a bottle tree on the lawn, placing three mistletoe seeds inside above a door, hanging a red-wrapped horseshoe, open end down, over the front door, or placing a line of salt around the house. Chances are, this last remedy will be the only one palatable to those like Frannie's mother, a former Ole Miss Chi Omega, who displays a true Southerner's serenity in the face of the supernatural, and would undoubtedly reject any suggestion to include bottle trees and blue windows as part of any remodeling plans!

MISSISSIPPI ON THE ATLANTIC

In the early to mid-1900s, many Mississippi river country blacks endured extreme poverty, unemployment, Jim Crow laws, segregation, and an impenetrable wall of racial prejudice. In response to these difficulties, they created legendary heroes who not only rejected the white man's legal and societal restrictions but also rose entirely above them. One such mythic figure was John Henry, who, in Tunica County, was reputed to have built the Delta's fabled Yellow Dog railroad. According to legend, John Henry could tote a bale of cotton under each arm or single-handedly lift a steamboat off a snag.

Another black mythic hero was "Shine," so called from the saying "so black he shines." Shine achieved legendary status as a fireman on the ill-fated liner *Titanic* who supposedly survived the ship's 1912 disaster. Flaunting white man's morality as the *Titanic* floundered in frigid North Atlantic waters, Shine "was in Sugar Ray's Bar drinking Seagram's Seven" as the terrified whites prepared to meet their Maker. When white women offered him sexual favors in exchange for his seat on a lifeboat, Shine declined their offers, saying, "One thing about you white folks I couldn't understand: y'all wouldn't offer me that [sex] when we was on land."

STAY AWAY FROM ME, STAGOLEE

The darker side of river-country black mythmaking involved the black antihero who, in his total rejection of the white man's value system, became a hardened, psychopathic killer. The most famous of these in the early 1900s was Delta badman "Stagolee." According to the legend, Stagolee once killed a man for stealing his Stetson hat and, after being executed for his crime, terrified the Devil by boldly exclaiming, "Stand back, Tom Devil, I'm gonna rule hell by myself!" Like Mississippi riverboatmen a century earlier, Stagolee even had his own brazen boast:

> Back in '32 when times was hard,
> I carried a sawed-off shotgun and a crooked deck of cards,
> Wore blue-suede shoes and carried a diamond cane . . .
> Had a six-inch knife with a bebop chain. . . .
> I'm that mean son of a bitch they call, "Stagolee."

THE DEVIL AT THE DELTA CROSSROADS

The Mississippi Delta's famous bluesmen, John Hurt, John Lee Hooker, James ("Son") Thomas, Muddy Waters, Howlin' Wolf, Son House, Willie Brown, Sam Chatmon, Willie Dixon, Big Joe Williams, Tommy Johnson, and Robert Johnson, gave the world this music form and also played a significant role in fathering rock-and-roll. The most influential of these "country bluesmen" may be Robert Johnson, not only for his extraordinary style but also for the means he reputedly devised to acquire it.

According to the legend, in 1929, a teenaged Johnson sought recognition from Clarksdale bluesmen Son House and Willie Brown by strumming his guitar outside a juke joint where the masters were playing. After several customers complained about the racket,

House ran Johnson off, telling the humiliated boy, "You can't play nothing." Johnson slipped quietly into the darkness and eased out of town.

Six months later, Johnson reappeared and accosted House and Brown during another of their engagements. Again taunted about his lack of ability, Johnson took House's seat and treated the two bluesmen to an eye-opening, jaw-dropping guitar performance. They later heard that Johnson had met the Devil at a crossroads near the Mississippi River town Beulah, in Bolivar County. There, Johnson had received his unearthly talent at the cost of his soul, which the Devil promised to take eight years later. As is often the case, the Devil got the best of the bargain, taking Johnson's soul eight years later in a juke-joint knife fight in Greenwood (many believe he was also poisoned), before Johnson's music had received the national acclaim it later garnered thanks to the popularity of Mississippi bluesman B. B. King.

Even so, Johnson knew great local success and never denied making the demonic deal. To the contrary, the quality of his music suggests the possibility of supernatural assistance. But the best evidence of Johnson's devilish deal may be found in the confessional tone of his song "Crossroad Blues," in which he begs for redemption and for a loophole in his Satanic contract:

> I went to the crossroad, fell down on my knees.
> Asked the Lord above, "Have mercy, now,
> Save poor Bob, if you please."

Chapter Eight

RIVER RATS IN RIVER TOWNS

Anyone thinking that the turn of the twentieth century brought an end to the Mississippi river country's supply of the extraordinary people and events for which it had become famous the preceding four centuries should certainly think again. "River rats," as river-country denizens are known to outsiders, were always cut from a uniquely flamboyant cloth, and the present age has done little to alter that. From mid-1800s characters such as Delta pioneer James A. Towne to early 1900s figures such as the heroic train engineer Casey Jones, the inventive Boy Who Saved Vicksburg, and the notorious outlaw Wild Bill Sullivan, many modern-day river rats left indelible marks on the pages of Deep South

Greek Revival style home, Grand Boulevard, Greenwood

history. As much as any other American region, the Mississippi river country continues to produce its share of intriguing tales, as well as a plenitude of troubadours and authors ready and willing to tell them well into the new millennium.

SORRY I ASKED

Pioneer James A. Towne came to the Yazoo River Delta in 1849, settling fifteen miles north of Greenwood in a tiny village known today as Minter City. He arrived with little more than a mule-drawn wagon and a few meager possessions, but soon purchased 10,000 acres of prime Delta farmland at twenty-five cents per acre. Called "Uncle Jimmy" by his neighbors, Towne mostly eschewed public life; he never filed a lawsuit, fought a fight, cast a vote, or served on a jury. However, he did support the growing Methodist Church by giving each newly arrived Minter City preacher a wagon and a mule.

In the American frontier tradition, Towne expected every man to carry his own weight, and the coming of the twentieth century did little to moderate that belief. So when one of Minter City's new Methodist preachers asked him to lead the congregation in prayer, Towne replied, "Pray yourself, preacher. That's what we pay you for!"

CHANGE OF LUCK AT MIDNIGHT

Undoubtedly, many visitors to rural Yazoo Delta plantations have secretly wished they could reside in such pastoral splendor. While such a wish may seem pie in the sky to most, two men made this dream a reality with little more than a wish; a card game was all it took. The first such event occurred in the mid-1800s near a bend of the Yazoo River between Yazoo City and Belzoni. There, two deer hunters camping in a swamp made a poker wager of part of a million-dollar cash inheritance against several hundred acres of rich Delta farmland. Jimmy Dick Hill won the hand, glanced at his watch, which read exactly 12:00 A.M., and exclaimed, "Well, boys, it's midnight, and that's just what I'm going to call my land—Midnight!"

Midnight Plantation was constructed on the very spot where Hill won the hand, and the town of Midnight later developed with the plantation as its focal point. Nowadays, Midnight's downtown area offers little more than a laundromat, post office, and combination snack shop, grocery, and recreation hall, prompting a former postmaster to quip, "Midnight is growing like a stump."

Rising Sun Plantation, located near Greenwood's southernmost city limits, was also won in a card game. This time, the game ended at dawn, hence the plantation's name. This raises the inevitable question that plantation-seeking gamblers must ask—what do you call a plantation won at 8:23 P.M. or 3:00 A.M.?

WAY DOWN UPON THE YAZOO RIVER?

Greenwood has always enjoyed the reputation of being one of the river country's most

"Big House," Florewood River Plantations State Park, Greenwood

enchantingly beautiful towns. With its brick streets paved in 1914, fifty-seven 1890s buildings comprising downtown's Cotton Row, stately Grand Boulevard lined with towering oaks and equally impressive Greek Revival, Queen Anne, and Victorian Gothic style mansions, Second Renaissance Revival courthouse with a four-faced clock tower, and ubiquitous foliage so well nurtured by the town's three rivers as to remind visitors of Ireland, Greenwood remains one of the world's loveliest cotton capitals.

Such was the case in the nineteenth century when Stephen Collins Foster strolled down River Road on the Yazoo River's banks in downtown Greenwood, taking note of the village's matchless pulchritude. He later penned a song that lauded the enchanting aspects of the town, "Way Down upon the Yazoo River, Far, Far Away." The song began with the following tribute:

> Way down upon the Yazoo River, far, far away,
> There's where my heart is turning ever;
> There's where the old folks stay.
> All up and down the whole creation, sadly I roam,
> Still longing for the old plantation
> and for the old folks at home.

Yazoo River, downtown Greenwood

When he later offered the manuscript for sale in Pittsburgh, a publisher offered to accept Foster's work on condition that he change the river's name, which, the publisher believed, would "make everyone laugh, thus spoiling the beauty and sentiment of the song." Over Foster's strenuous objections, the decision was made to use another name. Foster and his brother ultimately chose Florida's Swannee River as a replacement, even though Foster had never seen that river in person. Although the world-famous tune, "Way Down upon the Swannee River" or "Old Folks at Home," names a stream far, far away from the Yazoo River, its words still serve as a fitting ode to one of the loveliest of locales in the heart of the Mississippi river country.

THE TRAIN THAT WOULDN'T RUN

Eight miles east of Greenville and two miles north of Leland is the town of Stoneville, nowadays home to a major federal Agricultural Experimental Station. Back in the late 1870s, Stoneville suffered hard times occasioned by a vicious outbreak of malaria and several devastating fires. Fortunately for Stonevillians, a railroad line between Stoneville and Greenville kept their struggling community alive and transported passengers through the otherwise impassable Fish Lake Swamp.

Although the fare was quite reasonable at a mere one dollar, some passengers probably felt cheated for paying anything at all. The train often jumped its tracks, requiring the passengers to disembark and use logs to lift its cars back onto the track. Even when it encountered no difficulties, the Stoneville train traveled so slowly that if a passenger's hat blew off, he had time to hop off, recover his hat, and still overtake the train!

TRUE EQUALITY

Delta folks have always enjoyed the reputation of publicly expressing a fondness for liquor that greatly exceeds that admitted by their fellows in Mississippi's northeastern hills and central Piney Woods regions. And while the latter have sometimes looked askance at Delta intemperance, the former have occasionally poked public fun at their eastern neighbors' teetotaling habits. Such was the case in an 1880s Greenwood newspaper article that highlighted the differing viewpoints of Deltonians and Carroll County hillfolk where "the Devil's brew" was concerned:

> From the *Carrollton Conservative* [newspaper] we learn that in Carrollton, while gentlemen are charged initiation fees and dues in the temperance society, ladies are admitted free. In Greenwood we are satisfied that it would not be necessary to offer any such extra inducement to the ladies to forego the exhilarating beverage. In fact, we are quite sure that, on an average, the Greenwood ladies are no more firmly addicted to their cups than are the gentlemen.

CHAMPEEN O' THE WOODS

Like many river-country towns, south Mississippi's Hattiesburg is home to two rivers, the Bouie and the Leaf, which meet near U.S. Highway 11 northeast of the city. The highway runs southwest through the town until, just beyond the city limits, it passes by the place where America's greatest bare-knuckle boxer of all time, John L. Sullivan, defended his International Bare Knuckle Crown for the final time. On July 8, 1889, an insufferably hot 107-degree day, Sullivan duked it out with local hopeful Jake Kilrain in a seventy-five-round match that made Sullivan the last International Bare Knuckle Champion and landed all the participants in the local Hattiesburg jail.

New Orleans fight promoters and boxing fans had wanted the match in Louisiana, but the governor refused to allow it, even calling out the National Guard to prevent its occurrence. Then, while visiting New Orleans, Hattiesburgian Charlie Rich mentioned to several interested parties that a natural amphitheater near his home called Richburg Hill would be the ideal setting for the proposed match. New Orleans promoters promptly came to Hattiesburg and constructed a twenty-four-foot, sawdust-padded turf ring for the World Heavyweight Title bout featuring Sullivan and Kilrain. Mississippi's governor Robert Lowrey also attempted to block the fight by offering a $500 reward for the capture of the participants and by calling out the state militia to back up his ban. But the troops were "unable" to locate the fight despite the fact that it was attended by 3,000 screaming Louisiana and Mississippi fans.

The five-foot, ten-inch, 207-pound Sullivan didn't allow the negativity surrounding the event to dampen either his enthusiasm or his appetite. On July 7, he had a seven-pound sea bass, five eggs, a half-loaf of bread, six tomatoes, and tea for breakfast; steak and ale for lunch; and three chickens on a bed of rice for dinner. After rising at 5:30 the morning of the bout, he consumed a whole broiled chicken. Having successfully defended his title on the coast in Mississippi City back in 1882, Sullivan eagerly looked forward to a resumption of his good Magnolia State fortune. Weighing in at 183 pounds, the smaller Kilrain told friends that his strategy involved wearing down and outlasting his opponent with a "duck and run" approach. Fans poured into Hattiesburg by train, clamoring for the ten-dollar ringside tickets. They didn't have to wait very long, because at 10:15 A.M. the contestants came out slugging, but not in accordance with modern-day rules.

In those days, not only were the gloves missing, so was the bell. Under the London Prize Ring rules, rounds ended only with a knockdown and not before, usually lasting from one to fifteen minutes. With a thirty-second interval between rounds as the fighters' only respite, the match lasted until one man threw in the towel or was physically unable to continue the scrap. The refereeing was also a tad unconventional. This fight's referee, John Fitzpatrick, the former mayor of New Orleans, admitted after the fight that he "was too busy watching the principals to notice the fight."

Wearing colored tights, white stockings, and spiked shoes, Sullivan and Kilrain bloodied each other as best they could for two hours and sixteen minutes. Kilrain ended the first round in five seconds by knocking Sullivan down. After that, it was mostly Sullivan for seventy-four more rounds. He knocked down the challenger twenty-four times, threw him down seven, and shoved him down six, and Kilrain took twenty-six intentional falls to bring punishing rounds to an end. Sullivan knocked him out cold in the fourteenth and sixteenth rounds, but Kilrain gamely refused to strike Sullivan as the champ barfed up his chicken breakfast in the forty-fourth round. The nausea had little apparent effect on Sullivan, who cooled off between rounds with tea and brandy or beer.

The local sheriff also remained cool, agreeing not to stop the fight in return for Rich's offer of a front-row seat; he gamely agreed to arrest the fighters *after* the match. The fans standing around the ring endured greater difficulty with the 107-degree heat, being unable to leave their spots for fear of losing their position to others. Consequently, they were forced to pay the local boys' fee of one dollar for ringside delivery of glasses of water.

Kilrain's second finally threw in the towel after the challenger couldn't come out for the seventy-sixth round. Sullivan received the winner-take-all purse of $10,500, and the fans contributed $1,000 to Kilrain for his gallant effort. Both were arrested and indicted on charges of illegal prizefighting and assault and battery, while the referee was merely charged with aiding and assisting. They all avoided jail terms by paying fines ranging from $200 to $1,000.

This was the last International Bare Knuckle Championship fight, leaving Sullivan as the all-time Bare Knuckle king. He died at age fifty-nine, but not before donning the gloves and fighting thirty-seven more bouts under the new Marquis of Queensberry rules, winning twelve by knockout, twenty by decision, scoring three draws and one no decision, and suffering only one knockout. Kilrain survived into his eighties, once taking a punch at a fan who reminded him of his loss to Sullivan. To no one's surprise, Kilrain missed.

JOURNALISTIC INTEGRITY?

Anyone wondering how the media suddenly went to hell in a hand basket in the 1990s should consider this impressive example of 1800s journalistic casuistry. During the late 1890s, the New Orleans *Picayune* frequently published articles condemning Crescent City bare-knuckle boxing, labeling the sport a "grotesque" glorification of brute strength. After Mississippi's Governor Lowrey allowed the illegal Sullivan-Kilrain fight to take place near Hattiesburg, the *Picayune* took him to task for his failure to uphold the law. Of course, none of this stopped the paper from devoting 20,000 words and its first two pages to the Sullivan-Kilrain fight, prompting cries of hypocrisy from its readers.

Several days later, the *Picayune* responded with an editorial that questioned the *public's* sincerity in condemning the barbarous sport. The article read, in part:

> If public opinion were sincere, brutality would be driven from the ring. But the trouble is brutality is what is in request, and the people alone are to blame. . . . They demand brutality, and therefore the caterers of such amusements must bend to the popular will.

GRAVY TRAIN WRECK

Interest in gambling never waned in the river country, remaining popular everywhere from New Orleans to Memphis. It was still in full swing in 1900 Memphis, and whenever a Beale Street gambler was fortunate enough to clean out a house and break up a game, the losers would follow him around town and help him spend his winnings. These hangers-on were called "the gravy train" and, not surprisingly, were often given the runaround by those they were trailing. According to river-country folklore connoisseur B. A. Botkin, one winner led his gravy train all over Memphis by both buggy and streetcar into the wee hours of the morning, until the lone straggler finally said, "Brother, if you ain't goan' spend nuthin', nor goan' give me nuthin', I gotta ask you to please give me the fare to git back where I started!"

BETTER BY THE BOTTLE

Coca-cola, the classic American soft drink, was served entirely via soda fountains until 1894, when Vicksburger Joseph A. Biedenharn became the first to serve it in bottles from a little red-brick building called the Biedenharn Candy Company. The store still stands today in downtown Vicksburg, where you would test even Southern hospitality by showing up and ordering a Pepsi.

THE CASEY WHO DIDN'T STRIKE OUT

The Big Black River crosses under the Illinois Central Railroad near Vaughan, Mississippi, the town where John Luther ("Casey") Jones rode his iron horse into the pages of history. Originally hailing from Cayce (now Casey), Illinois, Jones caught the railroad bug in his teens, starting out as a telegrapher but ending up in his legendary role as engineer and brakeman. When the young engineer first met his wife to be, he "blushed to the roots of his hair" and married her after a whirlwind courtship. Her family soon dubbed him "Casey" after his hometown, and his growing reputation as one of Mississippi's greatest trainmen soon set the stage for his historic, heroic deed. It came during the wee hours of April 20, 1900, at the Vaughan ICRR depot.

On April 19, a stormy Sunday night, Casey and his northbound No. 382, a 4-6-0 McQueen Locomotive, arrived at Memphis's Poplar Street station en route from Canton, Mississippi. There he was informed that the southbound Cannonball Express run back to Canton had been canceled due to another engineer's illness. Needing extra cash to help move his new family from central Mississippi to Memphis, Casey volunteered not only to connect the No. 1 southbound Cannonball to his 382 and make the 188-mile "double out" return trip, he also agreed to make up the hour lost in order to get the train to Canton on time, or "on the advertised" in railroad jargon. Already known as an "artist with an engine" for his knack of taking curves at the highest possible speed, and for knowing when to pass up time-consuming water stops and still avoid having his engine run dry, Casey felt confident he could get No. 382 in "on the advertised" despite the inclement weather conditions.

Casey Jones Museum, Vaughan

A foggy, rainy night hampered visibility and nullified the effect of the train's kerosene headlight, but presented the ideal conditions for engine speed, allowing Jones to travel at speeds of 95 to 100 miles per hour. Commenting to his fireman, Sim Webb, about the good time No. 382 was making, Casey said, "Sim, the old girl's got her high-heeled slippers on tonight." By the time he'd reached Durant, Casey had made up all the lost time, but was informed during that stop of the slight possibility of a tangle of trains up ahead at the Vaughan depot.

When Casey arrived north of the Vaughan depot, southbound No. 83 had been almost completely rerouted onto another track, but an airbrake hose had popped on another train, freezing its wheels and preventing No. 83 from completely exiting Casey's line. Four of its cars loaded with hay and corn still remained on Casey's track. Although a flagman tried to signal Casey 3,000 feet before the depot, the engineer remained unaware of the logjam until Sim Webb cried, "Look out, we're gonna hit something!" Casey was positioned on the other side of the train from Webb and couldn't see No. 83's caboose, but he yelled for Webb to jump, threw on the emergency brake, shut off the throttle, and slammed the gears into reverse. This slowed the train's speed from seventy-five to thirty-five miles per hour and saved the passengers and crew. But the crash killed Casey instantly and sent No. 382's engine off the tracks and onto its side, although the four passenger cars never left the track.

The Illinois Central Railroad paid Webb $5 for body bruises, compensated the depot messenger with $23 for back injuries, and paid a passenger $1 for being "shaken up." The total damages were $3,324, including $1,396 for Casey's No. 382. Casey's noble sacrifice achieved national acclaim when a reporter on board ran the story in newspapers across the land. One of Casey's Canton friends, an African-American engine wiper named Wallace Sanders, composed "The Ballad of Casey Jones," which became a national hit in 1909. Sanders never received a penny of the hit song's proceeds, although the record producer did give him a bottle of gin for his efforts. But the song's subject, the immortal Casey Jones, achieved legendary status that endures to this day, forever preserved in the ballad that plays continuously at the Casey Jones Museum State Park in Vaughan.

THE HATE WHITE CHIEF

When John Sharp Williams retired from congressional service, he bemoaned the coming of the Populists, led in Mississippi by one "Vardaman." The Vardaman of whom Williams wrote was the handsome, flamboyant, early-1900s demagogue James Kimble Vardaman, known by his backwoods supporters as the "Great White Chief." This Greenwood newspaperman wore long black hair, a wide cowboy hat, a white flannel suit, and a red necktie symbolizing his allegiance to the poor, white common people, or "rednecks," as he affectionately termed them.

A staunch advocate of the separation of the races, Vardaman supported the repeal of the Fourteenth and Fifteenth Amendments to the U.S. Constitution and opposed granting rights of first-class citizenship to African-Americans. Like Williams, Vardaman also detested Pres. Teddy Roosevelt's economic policies, but Vardaman further objected to Roosevelt's sincere, publicly expressed desire to alleviate the terrible suffering endured by American blacks. When Roosevelt invited Booker T. Washington to a social event at the White House, Vardaman penned several scathing editorials in his own newspaper, the *Greenwood Commonwealth*. However, neither Vardaman's poetry nor his prose exhibited the wit and charm of John Sharp Williams'. To the contrary, it displayed Vardaman's natural vulgarity and grotesquely racist perspective.

When Mississippi governor Longino invited Roosevelt to Mississippi for a 1902 bear hunt, Vardaman ran the following ad in the *Commonwealth,* designed to denigrate the president for his alleged intention of socially mixing the races:

> WANTED—Sixteen big fat, mellow, rancid 'coons' to sleep with Roosevelt when he comes down to go bear hunting with our governor Longy.

After Roosevelt departed Mississippi, Vardaman ran this grotesque poem in his editorial column:

> Teddy has come and Teddy has gone,
> and the lick spittle spittled and the fawning did fawn.
> The coons smelt as loud as a musk rat's nest,
> And Teddy licked his chops and said it smelt the best.

Later, in 1903, Vardaman launched his most scathing attack on the president, derogatorily referring to Roosevelt's mother in another of his *Commonwealth* editorials:

> Probably old lady Roosevelt, during the period of gestation, was frightened by a dog, and that fact may account for the qualities of the male pup which are so prominent in Teddy. I wouldn't do her an injustice, but I am disposed to apologize to the dog for mentioning it.

Despite their mutual dislike for TR, Vardaman and Williams disagreed violently on most racial issues, especially that of African-American citizens' right to a public education. Williams and other planter-statesmen, including the venerable L. Q. C. Lamar, supported public education for blacks. Conversely, Vardaman and his followers strongly opposed black education, enfranchisement, and employment opportunities. These disagreements led to a 1907 contest between then governor Vardaman and Williams for one of Mississippi's two U.S. Senate seats. Williams won the seat, but the battle between the Vardaman "rednecks" and the Delta planter-statesmen camp was only just heating up.

LIAR NOT A CHEAT

When Mississippi's other U.S. senator, Anslem McLaurin, died in December of 1909, it fell to the Mississippi legislature to select a replacement until the 1911 general election. It was decided that the vote would be tallied in the state house by secret ballot to avoid placing undue political pressure on legislators. Vardaman's supporters, who sought to apply a lion's share of that pressure, derisively branded the election as the "Secret Caucus of 1910."

The field included Vardaman and six men united in their common desire to prevent Vardaman's election. After fifty-seven votes failed to produce a majority winner, Vardaman's opponents finally selected wealthy Greenville planter and railroad attorney LeRoy Percy as their candidate. Percy defeated Vardaman on the fifty-eighth ballot, eighty-seven to eighty-two.

But the Vardaman forces were not willing to let the matter drop. One legislator, Theodore G. Bilbo, began publicly slurring his comrades who had voted for Percy, alleging that many had taken bribes. One falsely accused legislator, Leland lawyer Eugene Gerald, sent word to Bilbo that if he showed his face in Washington County after dark, "it would be for the last time." The controversy went nuclear when Bilbo admitted that he himself had been bribed to vote for Percy. He had taken the money, Bilbo declared, only to keep it as evidence of the crime. A special grand jury was convened to handle the fallout and finally decide the delicate matter. Although the man accused of bribing Bilbo was no political ally of Percy's, everyone knew he hated Vardaman even more. But after Bilbo turned the "bribe" money over to the grand jury, the district attorney discovered that many of the bills had been issued *after* the date of the election! Bilbo's claim was then disallowed, and Percy promptly took his Senate seat.

Although Bilbo and Vardaman ultimately became two of America's most notorious politicians, their opponent, LeRoy Percy, is remembered not only as a member of that rare breed of basically honest politicians but also as the patriarch of a family that greatly contributed to the river-country's literary reputation. Such men and women as his son William Alexander Percy, his cousin Walker Percy, and other river country writers—William Faulkner, Eudora Welty, Tennessee Williams, Shelby Foote, Hodding Carter II, Ellen Douglas, Stark Young, Willie Morris, Richard Wright, Barry Hannah, Beth Henley, Margaret Walker Alexander, Richard Ford, Ellen Gilchrist, Charles Wilson, Thomas Hal Phillips, Martin Hegwood, Lewis Hordan, Greg Iles, John Grisham—have not only established their region as the preeminent seat of twentieth-century American literature, drama, and popular fiction, they have also striven nobly to set the record straight as to who wore the white and black hats during Mississippi's most troubled political times.

BUT LIES ARE MIGHTIER THAN THE PEN

Unfortunately, Senator Percy's 1910 victory did not end Vardaman and Bilbo's careers, or even delay their ascendance for any substantial length of time. The very next year, Vardaman defeated Percy in the 1911 senatorial election, and this ushered in an era that some historians have labeled "the Rise of Democracy" but others have termed "the Revolt of the Rednecks." However it's called, it saw the preeminence of such men as Vardaman and Bilbo in Mississippi politics for the next half-century. In his book, *Lanterns on the Levee,* LeRoy Percy's son, lawyer and poet William Alexander Percy, said of Vardaman and

Bilbo's supporters that "they were the sort of people that lynch Negroes, that mistake hood-lumism for wit, and cunning for intelligence, that attend revivals and fight and fornicate in the bushes afterwards." Vardaman and Bilbo laughed all the way to the bank, both serving several terms as governor and U.S. senator during the next forty years.

Theodore G. Bilbo, known to his supporters as "the Man," advocated sending all blacks back to Africa and building streets with bricks so the bricks could be dug up and turned over when worn down. A short, bulldog of a man, Bilbo was much given to race-baiting hyperbole, once publicly referring to an opponent as "a cross between a hyena and a mongrel . . . begotten in a nigger graveyard at midnight, suckled by a sow and educated by a fool." Of the African-American citizen, Bilbo frequently declared him to be "only a hundred and fifty years removed from the jungle and eatin' his own kind."

Such comments soon drew the ire of Greenville's progressive editor of the *Delta Democrat Times,* Hodding Carter, and touched off verbal volleys the likes of which were not seen again in the Mississippi river country until 1998, when WLBT-TV's flamboyant, African-American CEO Frank Melton took on the allegedly crooked Jackson city council-man Louis Armstrong and several other controversial black politicians. But unlike the Melton/city council conflict, which frequently featured good humor and quick wit, the Bilbo-Carter affair involved the most extreme, bloodcurdling invective imaginable.

Carter, whose editorials opposing racism and religious intolerance won him the 1946 Pulitzer Prize, went on the attack against Bilbo later that same year after Bilbo, whose gubernatorial administration had left the state in $12,000,000 debt in 1932, announced his intentions to seek a third term as U.S. senator. In a scathing editorial, Carter declared that "Bilbo's mind is so soaked in the poisonous slime of his bigotry that it reminds us of noth-ing so much as a neglected cesspool." Three days later Carter called Bilbo a "dirty minded little office seeker."

Taking a break from his vicious attacks upon blacks, Jews, and Catholics, Bilbo labeled the newspaperman as "this miserable little Quisling who has sunken deeper in his perfid-ious course of betraying the white race and our glorious Southland." Carter was, accord-ing to Bilbo, "as bitter an enemy to our customs, practices, ideals, and ways of life as any Russian refugee that ever landed in New York . . . [and has] joined hands with the Negroes, Communists, and foreigners in a studied and determined effort to smear and destroy me." Bilbo even condemned Carter for winning a Pulitzer Prize, charging that no "red-blooded Southerner . . . would accept a Poolizter-blitzer prize given by a bunch of nigger-loving, Yankeefied communists for editorials advancing the mongrelization of the race."

Carter responded that if Bilbo was a Southern patriot, he was "happy to be called a Quisling." The newspaperman boldly answered Bilbo's charge that he was a "nigger lover," proudly admitting, "I try to love all my fellowmen—Negroes, Jews, Catholics, and all those Bilbo has tried to humiliate, down to, but not including, Bilbo himself. Not even God Almighty could stretch his compassion that far."

Despite Carter's efforts, Bilbo won a close vote in the Democrat primary of 1946, thereby assuring himself victory in the general election. Although the pen has often proved mightier than the sword, in this case, at least, lies had proved mightier than the pen. Even so, Carter is now remembered as the quintessential muckraking journalist, while history recalls Bilbo in an entirely different light. This viewpoint was eloquently stated by one of Carter's fellow journalists, Fred Sullens, who upon Bilbo's demise penned a most fitting epitaph for the Man:

> Beneath this stone old Theo lies;
> Nobody laughs and nobody cries;
> Where he's gone or how he fares;
> Nobody knows, and nobody cares.

DON'T WANT TO BE YOUR TEDDY BEAR

Despite Vardaman and Bilbo's efforts to keep him at arm's length, Pres. Theodore Roosevelt came to Mississippi on November 14, 1902, to hunt black bear on the edge of the game-rich Delta. The president made camp in Smedes, a tiny village located twenty-four miles north of Vicksburg on the banks of the Sunflower River. Also in attendance were several other notables, including local planters Hugh L. Foote and W. W. Mangum, famed Rough Rider Lt. John L. McElhenney, and the region's leading bear tracker, Holt Collier. Collier, a black Civil War scout who had served under Confederate general Wade Hampton, was the area's bear-hunt guide *extraordinaire,* having been in on over sixteen hundred previous bear kills.

The party also requested the use of a local black man's famous bear hounds for the expedition, but the old man was unimpressed with the presidential messenger's request, saying, "I don't give a damn if Booker T. Washington wants them, he can't get my dogs less'n I comes along. Understand?" Despite having to endure such occasional incidents of local impertinence, Roosevelt joyfully immersed himself in the event, saying, "I'm not here as the president, but as a bear hunter, and all hunters—black and white—will mess from the same pot."

After Roosevelt failed to bag a relatively smallish 235-pound bear known to inhabit the area, Holt took matters into his own hands. He hunted the beast down, rendered it unconscious with a rifle butt, tied it to a tree, and summoned the president to the kill. But Roosevelt gamely refused the easy trophy, not only for himself but everyone in the party. Contrary to popular belief, the press was not in attendance at the time, having been kept at bay by a steadfast black camp guard, Freedman Wallace. While keeping the journalists out of camp, Wallace had responded to a newspaperman's assertion that "you've got no legal right to stop me" by tapping the barrel of his shotgun and saying, "This is the only law we know."

Nevertheless, the press soon got wind of Roosevelt's merciful act, and articles and cartoons began appearing all over the nation, lauding the great white hunter's benevolence.

Young Southerners love their teddy bears

A Brooklyn toy manufacturer capitalized on the story by creating a lovable little toy he called the "Teddy Bear." The item proved a smashing success with the kiddies and soon became Western civilization's most popular children's toy.

THE BOY WHO SAVED VICKSBURG

When Eudora Welty said that time was important to Mississippians because "it has dealt with us . . . we have suffered and learned and progressed through it," she was certainly speaking of Vicksburg. Although its hardships during the Civil War siege are its most well known, Vicksburg has endured a timeless spate of deadly troubles. In 1835, Vicksburgers waged a war with riverboat gamblers resulting in several deaths and five lynchings. They took on some rowdy flatboatmen later that year, but bloodshed was averted when the riverboatmen got the town soldiers so drunk and so enthralled them with tall river tales that the vigilantes forgot the purpose of their mission and let the riverboatmen leave in peace. After the war left Vicksburg in a shambles, a fire sacked the town in 1866, and in 1875, a skirmish between local whites and black Reconstruction officials claimed the lives of sixteen residents. And then things really took a turn for the worse.

In 1878 a yellow-fever epidemic claimed over fifteen hundred victims, but the worst news had already arrived in 1876, when the Mississippi River changed its course and left the former "Gibraltar of the Confederacy" high and dry. Faced with the same extinction suffered by numerous other commercial river towns deserted by the Father of Waters, Vicksburgers prepared for the worst.

But tragedy was averted thanks to a young boy who, along with his friends, had often fished the chain of lakes running between the Yazoo River and Vicksburg. He suggested to town officials that they cut a channel through the lakes that would divert the Yazoo's path and bring it into the old Mississippi River bed, connecting the Yazoo and Mississippi within Vicksburg city limits. City officials approved the idea and engaged a contingent of engineers to do the work, and by December 22, 1902, Vicksburgers once more enjoyed the thriving river trade the river gods had sought to deny them.

Although floods in 1922 and 1927 took a terrible toll, and a 1953 tornado caused thirty-eight more deaths, Vicksburgers never doubted that they would overcome those disasters. After all, their city had already survived the mighty Mississippi's best effort to destroy it, thanks to their imaginative, youthful hero—The Boy Who Saved Vicksburg.

REAP WHAT YOU SOW

As had been the case with Natchez' Lorenzo ("Crazy") Dow in the early 1800s, con artists posing as "soul-saving" preachers continued to plague the river-country populace well into the twentieth century. A perfect example was one "sanctified" sister named Cindy Mitchell, who once tried to pull a fast one on her Greenwood flock by promising to walk on the waters of the Yalobusha River. Unbeknownst to her congregation, the preacher had earlier erected a wooden walkway just below water level that stretched several yards out into the river. With her flock waiting expectantly on the Yalobusha's shores, Mitchell had herself paddled out into the muddy waters to locate the platform.

But the river had either risen high above the platform or washed it away entirely. Like Dow before her, Mitchell was not to be outdone by a twist of fate (or God's sense of justice) and bravely debarked on shore, saying, "I ain't goin' to walk. The Lawd Himsef done said, 'Don't do it, Cindy, not befo' folks who ain't got the faith of a mustard seed!'" But the river-country folk were not so gullible as their forebears had been a hundred years earlier, and Cindy Mitchell's congregation, much as had the Yalobusha River, soon left her high and dry.

SHE BLEWITT

Pronounced like "slaughter," the tiny hamlet of Schlater is located eighteen miles north-west of Greenwood. How the local citizenry came up with the town's name is a vintage Mississippi Delta tale of love, loss, and land.

Randall Blewitt was wealthy enough to garner the privilege of naming the village in which he lived, so he named it "Maryland," after his fiancée, Mary Means. And when he left Maryland to join the Confederate army, Major Blewitt asked his brother to take good care of his beloved. Much to Blewitt's chagrin, his brother took better care of Mary than he had envisioned, asking for her hand in marriage after receiving word that Randall had been badly injured at the Battle of Manassas. Understandably miffed at his fiancée's premature acceptance of his brother's proposal, the seriously wounded Blewitt changed his will and left 889 prime Delta acres to his nephew, Randall Blewitt Schlater. When, in 1911, the younger Schlater donated 89 of those acres to his hometown, its leaders changed the village's name from Maryland to Schlater, a classic last-laugh coup for Randall.

RAPPERS' DOZEN DELIGHTS

Anyone noticing the aggressive, abusive language so prevalent in today's popular rap music may assume that rap lyrics are entirely the product of our present-day society's values. But modern-day values may not be the sole cause of rap music's saucy lyrics. According to historian James C. Cobb, "ritual insult was widely practiced in west Africa" and was adopted by African-American sharecroppers in early 1900s Mississippi to help alleviate the stress accompanied by the "constant humiliation and abuse" showered upon them by white law and society. Lacking any avenue for expressing aggression against whites, some blacks released that aggression via humorous insults towards their own people.

According to Cobb, this river-country practice was known as "the dozens" and produced such lyrics as

> Your breath smell like a gallon of gas
> Or a cool breeze off a cheese's ass.

Sharecropper's shotgun house, Mississippi Delta

The connection between "the dozens" and modern rap is readily apparent, with the understanding that modern artistic license allows rappers to criticize all races, creeds, colors, and governmental authority figures in a spirit of equality and abuse for all.

MACHINE GUN KELLY GETS AN "A"

During the 1920s and 1930s, one of America's most notorious gangsters was Memphian George ("Machine Gun") Kelly. But in 1917, Kelly was little more than a poor student who had flunked out of Memphis's Central High School. Although such lapses usually terminated most academic careers, on September 20, 1917, Mississippi A&M (now Mississippi State University) accepted Kelly as a "special [probationary] student" in the school of agriculture. Before he withdrew from A&M on January 27, 1918, Kelly received a 0 in mechanical engineering, a 79 in personal hygiene, and an incomplete in military science. He also collected a total of 55 demerits during his short time in Starkville before eloping to Clarksdale with A&M coed Geneva Ramsey.

After divorcing Ramsey, Kelly entered the bootlegging business but reportedly "drank more of his bootleg hootch than he peddled." He then married Kathryn Shannon, whose parents ran a "fugitive farm" where criminals on the lam hid out at a cost of fifty dollars

1974 gangster reenactment, river-country style

per night. Kathryn gave Kelly his very first machine gun, and he learned to fire the weapon accurately by shooting walnuts off fence posts. He often impressed his new wife by writing his name in bullet holes on walls and fences. Although the heavyset, six-foot-tall gangster was often described as "not tough" and "very stupid," he nevertheless got all As in bank robbery and enjoyed more favorable press than Baby Face Nelson, Ma Barker, or Bonnie and Clyde.

He pulled a few heists in Mississippi, including the November 28, 1932, robbery of the Tupelo Citizens Bank, which netted him and four other bandits a total of $17,500 cash. The bank's manager told reporters that the robbery had been "planned to perfection" and informed police that the submachine-gun-toting robbers wore no masks, were quite calm, exhibited no sign of nervousness, and "cursed very little and seemed to be well mannered."

Kelly, who never killed anyone during his heists, was finally captured along with his wife in a small Memphis cottage on September 26, 1933. Surrendering without a fight, Kelly told the police, "I've been waiting on you all night." He was condemned to a life sentence at Alcatraz, and after a transfer to Leavenworth, died of a heart attack there in 1954.

TRESPASSERS WILL BE SHOT, KNIFED, OR REQUIRED TO HUNT

South of Mize, Mississippi, in a ten-square-mile area of Smith County between the Okatoma and Cohey creeks, lies Sullivan's Hollow, the home of the river country's most beloved outlaw, Wild Bill Sullivan. Like Dodge City's Wild Bill, Sullivan was tall, lean, suntanned, and mustachioed, wore a wide-brimmed hat, and carried two pistols and a knife in his belt. But he operated on a different side of the law from Marshal Hickok, fighting duels for personal satisfaction and bullying traveling salesmen and other unfortunate visitors to the Hollow. During 1905, the year Wild Bill Sullivan's sole murder conviction was reversed by the state supreme court, a newspaper reported that, during the past twenty years, forty people had died in Sullivan's Hollow feuds, making Kentucky's notorious Hatfield-McCoy affair seem minor by comparison!

Affectionately known by his neighbors as the King of the Hollow, the usually affable Sullivan was given a wide berth by strangers, and anyone who crossed him, especially while he was drinking, usually wound up knifed, shot, or missing. He met his match only once, when clever Itta Bena judge Mac Kimbrough figured out an unusual way to stop Wild Bill and his kin from burning out railroad trestles. Everyone in the Hollow knew Sullivan was responsible for the trestle vandalism, but no one could catch him in the act, and even fewer really wanted to be the first one on his block to do so. Judge Kimbrough solved the problem by going hunting with Wild Bill and *paying him $500* to stop burning the trestles. A man of his word, Sullivan never burned another trestle after taking the judge's bribe.

Until Wild Bill died in 1932, the people of the Hollow continued their wild and wooly ways. In 1902, a gunfight broke out during a preliminary hearing in Raleigh, and after over a hundred bullets whizzed through the air, one man, a mule, and a dog lay dead. As late as 1922, a Sullivan was accidentally killed during a gunfight that started over the controversial outcome of a Magee-Mize high-school basketball game! There was, it seems, only one truly "lead-proof" Sullivan, the one the Hollow people called Wild Bill.

NOMENCULTURE

In addition to reigning as some of America's most beautiful villages, many river-country towns sport names that make visiting map readers stop and stare. Where, they ask themselves, could anyone have dreamed up such names as Chunky, Biloxi (pronounced Bih-LUCK-see), Hot Coffee, D'Lo, Soso, Duck Hill, Alligator, and Hard Times? Some, like Alligator, Eden, and Hard Times, pretty much speak for themselves. Soso came from an answer to the question, "How are you feeling?" Many are derived from Indian names, such as Byhalia (white oak), Shuqualak (hog-wallow), Tupelo (to scream), Itta Bena (home in the woods), Senatobia (rest to the weary), Winona (first-born daughter), and Biloxi (broken pot).

Other towns have more conventional bases for their names. Chunky was named for a Choctaw Indian game, Belzoni took its name from Italian archeologist Giovanni Battista Belzoni, and Duck Hill was christened for a warlike Choctaw chief. Kosciusko and Carrollton were named for Revolutionary War heroes, but Guntown derived its name from the colonial Tory who founded the town. Some of the names are descriptive, such as Sandy Hook, named for a bend in the Pearl River, and Rosedale, a lasting tribute to the lovely, Mississippi River-nurtured rose gardens abundant throughout that Delta hamlet.

The two most interesting river-town names may be Hot Coffee and D'Lo. After the Civil War, J. J. Davis built a general store from which he sold an exceedingly tasty cup of coffee with molasses drippings. The store was located in Leaf River country about fifteen miles southwest of Soso. The locals honored his delicious brand by measuring the distance from where they were to Davis's store as "only so many more miles to hot coffee." When a town sprung up around the store, the people named it after the locale's most popular product.

Situated on the Strong River's banks, D'Lo is the quintessential sleepy Southern town. Nevertheless, the origin of its name does, on occasion, stir up a little controversy amongst the residents. Some believe it came from the French term de l'eau, meaning "some water" or "of the water," and was later corrupted by Anglo-American settlers. Others hold to the theory that early railroaders laying track through the region often remarked that the place was "too damn low" to avoid frequent flooding. Whatever the original basis for D'Lo's name, it was ultimately chosen from a list submitted by the U.S. Post Office Department. But anyone informing the good people of D'Lo that their town got its name from such a pedestrian source as a post-office list may discover what is meant by the river-country phrase "raisin' a ruckus"!

THE SINGING BRAKEMAN

The Mississippi river country has produced many chart-topping singers, including Faith Hill, Mose Allison, Ace Cannon, B. B. King, Bobbie Gentry, John Lee Hooker, the Staples Singers, Jerry Butler, Muddy Waters, LeAnn Rimes, Sam Cooke, Jimmy Buffett, Bo

Diddley, Steve Fobert, Pete Fountain, W. C. Handy, Denise LaSalle, Ike Turner, David Ruffin, Leontyne Price, Charlie Pride, Rufus Thomas, Conway Twitty, O. B. McClinton, and Moe Bandy. It also gave the world the King of Rock-and-Roll, Elvis Presley, the Bluesmaster for the Ages, Robert Johnson, and, last but not least, the Father of Country Music, Meridian's Jimmie Rodgers.

Growing up in the heart of Chickasawhay River country, Rodgers burst on the national music scene with his recordings of "Sleep Baby Sleep" and "Blue Yodel No. 1" in 1927. His national popularity thus assured, Rodgers traveled the country giving performances of such hits as "Mule Skinner Blues" and "Honeycomb," usually dressed in a light-colored suit, bow tie, and boater hat. In concert, he occasionally wore his uniform from when he was employed by the railroad, which earned him the nickname "The Singing Brakeman." Rodgers' unprecedented style—an energetic blend of country, yodeling, and blues, delivered in an emotional, plaintive voice—resulted in the sale of 20,000,000 records between 1927 and 1933.

It was, however, Rodgers' extraordinary courage that made him one of the river country's most beloved sons. After the early 1930s depression forced him back into hustling for paying jobs, and in poor health, the severely weakened Rodgers endured several excruciating days of recording sessions to produce twelve records that would ensure his wife and daughter's lasting financial security. His condition forced him to rest on a cot between sessions and sit propped on pillows before the microphone. Two days after completing the recordings, Jimmy Rodgers, aged thirty-six, died of tuberculosis in a New York City hotel room. Having already given the form and direction to country music necessary to ensure its success as a popular American music style, Rodgers bravely hastened his own demise to provide his family with the security they needed to survive America's Great Depression. He may not be the King, but he'll always be remembered as a Mississippi river-country saint.

ADVISE AND DISSENT

Despite the wit and wisdom routinely displayed by Mississippi river-country writers, they have rarely been asked to serve as counselors to the public, at least not with the frequency of other American pundits such as newspaper columnists Abigail Van Buren and Ann Landers, college professor and Internet adviser Camille Paglia, author and magazine columnist Florence King, or even beloved backwoods humorist Will Rogers. Upon pondering this conundrum, some argue that the river country's sages think too deeply to advise the common people, while others maintain that these hardworking novelists are just too swamped to take on the extra work. The more likely explanation is that our river-country wits are not at all shy about handing out advice; their advice is simply too cynical to print.

The perfect cases in point are the river country's two greatest writers and world-class curmudgeons, Mark Twain and William Faulkner. Twain, i.e., Samuel Clemens, lived an exciting life on the Mississippi River, and his far-flung adventures prompted him to give historians and journalists some dubious advice: "First get the facts, then you can distort them." He also eloquently addressed the general state of the human condition: "Of the demonstrably wise there are but two—those who commit suicide and those who keep their reasoning faculties atrophied with drink."

Faulkner, who lived a less adventurous life in tiny Oxford, Mississippi, and numerous Delta hunting camps, often offered advice of a more personal nature, much of it concerning hearth and home. In a Parisian interview he declared that "if a writer has to rob his mother, he will not hesitate; the *Ode to a Grecian Urn* is worth any number of old ladies." According to his biographer, Frederick R. Karl, Faulkner also volunteered to offer marital advice to thrice-divorced fellow-novelist Ernest Hemingway, and to warn his colleague against the evils of marriage, which Faulkner believed were more difficult for a man to resist than booze, drugs, or nose picking.

But despite their carefully woven cynical smokescreens, Twain and Faulkner proved to be devoted fathers, and not such intolerable husbands that their wives were forced to choose Twain's more radical option for the "demonstrably wise" (although Faulkner's wife, Estelle, grew understandably fond of her afternoon toddy after years of marriage to the Nobel Laureate many Oxford residents nicknamed "Count No 'Count").

And although they never achieved fame as lonely-hearts advice columnists, William Faulkner and Mark Twain certainly held their own as novelists and short-story authors.

Faulkner's home, Rowan Oak, Oxford

Chapter Nine

MODERN MARVELS

The Mississippi river country continues to produce its share of modern-day marvels, from great sports heroes such as Archie Manning and Walter Payton to courageous harbingers of social change such as journalist Hazel Brannon Smith and civil-rights activist James Meredith. Although this region is unsurpassed in natural beauty, abundant wildlife, and twenty-first-century opportunities, its other natural resource, its always hospitable, frequently flamboyant, and occasionally histrionic people, are the ladle that stirs this intriguing American melting pot. Love them or leave them, you'll never forget the time you spent being delighted, entertained, or even challenged in that distinctive river-country style!

Ventress Hall (1889), Ole Miss campus

MY KARMA RAN OVER YOUR DOGMA

One of the Deep South's greatest heroes is James Meredith, who, in support of equal rights for African Americans, suffered a bullet wound during a 1966 civil-rights march and kicked off Mississippi collegiate integration by enrolling as a student at the University of Mississippi in 1962. Several all-black Mississippi colleges existed as a matter of need in the early 1960s because African-Americans were not allowed entry into the University of Mississippi, Mississippi State University, or Mississippi Southern College (later University of Southern Mississippi) during that era. University and college segregation was so entrenched in Mississippi that Mississippi State refused to participate in several NCAA National Championship Basketball Tournaments because they refused to mix with integrated teams, and Mississippi Southern officials had Clyde Kennard sentenced to jail for seven years for applying for admission to Southern in 1959. But despite such dogged resistance, and often at the risk of his own life, Meredith insisted upon attending college in Yocona River country at Ole Miss, the state university he considered to be Mississippi's best.

Although university officials initially refused his enrollment, they eventually decided to honor President Kennedy's request for a peaceful submission to the Supreme Court's mandate to open their doors to Meredith. However, Gov. Ross Barnett, with the aid of universities board of trustees member M. M. Roberts, took control of the institution and prevented Meredith's admission. Over the objections of progressive Mississippi journalists, Ole Miss student newspaper editors, university president J. D. Williams, and board of trustees member Verner Holmes, Barnett fanned the flames of racism and whipped the hardcore rednecks and would-be Klansmen into a violent secessionist frenzy. This led to a redneck invasion of the campus and the death-dealing riot that accompanied Meredith's fall enrollment; of the 210 rioters arrested, only 25 were actually Ole Miss students.

As has happened throughout recorded history, even this unmitigated travesty produced one unexpectedly humorous incident. When Meredith and a white government official approached Governor Barnett, who stood blocking their path to the Lyceum's enrollment area, the double-dealing governor coolly asked, "Which one of you fellows is Mr. Meredith?" Ultimately, wiser heads prevailed, especially after prominent Ole Miss alumnus William H. Mounger and 127 other Jackson businessmen issued a public statement urging Mississippians to take a "sane [and] sensible" approach to Meredith's enrollment.

Thanks in large part to James Meredith's tenacity and perseverance, all of Mississippi's public colleges and universities soon opened their doors to African-American students, and public-high-school integration proved a great success nine years later. Today, Mississippi schools produce more per-capita black leaders than any other state and, since the 1970s, the University of Mississippi has won numerous national awards, including the Peterson Award, for outstanding minority recruitment and participation. And Meredith continues to pursue his against-the-grain destiny, supporting Ole Miss and actively campaigning for local

Republican candidates, who, he says (to the consternation of many welfare-state-supporting Democrats), offer a better future to hardworking citizens of all races, creeds, and colors.

While Martin Luther King, Jr., Rosa Parks, and Malcolm X continue to receive much deserved recognition as three of twentieth-century America's greatest heroes, the record should also reflect that Medgar Evers, Fannie Lou Hamer, and James Meredith are three Mississippi heroes whose personal sacrifices and lifelong contributions to American justice and equality remain unsurpassed in both America's and the Mississippi river country's annals of civil-rights achievement.

BRINGIN' DOWN THE HAMER

One of the most intriguing stories arising from the great civil-rights struggles of the 1960s was that of Sunflower River country hero Fannie Lou Hamer's one-woman battle to depose Jim Crow. The youngest of twenty children and a Delta sharecropper from the age of six, Hamer was unaware that blacks even had the right to vote until her forty-fifth year. When she attempted to register in 1962, she was denied by virtue of the infamous Constitution interpretation test, and the Sunflower County sheriff arrested her bus driver for having "too much yellow" on his bus, leaving Hamer and several other women stranded on the roadway. When she finally returned to the Marlow plantation where she had labored for the past eighteen years, she was given the boot and set adrift in what her employer assumed would be a drowning pool of poverty and unemployment. Undaunted, Hamer promptly took up the gauntlet and set out to free her people from the suffering and injustice they had endured throughout much of the last hundred years.

Working with the Student Non-Violent Coordinating Committee (SNCC), Hamer traversed the river country, giving speeches in support of black education and voter registration. Despite being assessed (and having her husband arrested for) a $9,000 water bill on a house with no running water, receiving volumes of hate mail, and enduring frequent threats against her life, and in spite of the general climate of fear occasioned by Medgar Evers' 1963 assassination and the 1964 murders of three Philadelphia civil-rights workers, Hamer remained steadfast in her mission. "Sometimes," she said, "it seems like to tell the truth today is to run the risk of being killed. But if I fall, I'll fall five feet four inches forward in the fight for freedom. I'm not backing off from that and no one will have to cover the ground I walk as far as freedom is concerned."

When attempting to represent Mississippi at the 1963 Democratic Convention, and when faced with unacceptable compromise measures supported by so-called liberals such as Lyndon Johnson and Hubert Humphrey, Hamer highlighted a speech to the credentials committee with the question, "Is this America, the land of the free and home of the brave where we have to sleep with our telephones off the hook because our lives be threatened daily because we want to live as decent human beings?"

Her grassroots methods and down-home wisdom ultimately proved more than a match for her opponents, ubiquitous and all powerful as they were. She answered charges of being a communist by saying that she knew as much about communism as "a horse do about Christmas." Once, when Ruleville's Mayor Charles Dorough attempted to exhaust Hamer's supply of free food and materials for the poor by announcing on the radio that "everyone" should go to her house, Hamer led the new arrivals in a voting-rights seminar! She also filed numerous school desegregation and local election lawsuits, gave seminars on how to pass voter-registration tests, pushed for investigations of racially motivated crimes, helped found an African-American-owned bank, and continued to meet with national civil-rights leaders Malcolm X, Andrew Young, and Harry Belafonte in support of equal rights for all United States citizens.

Before her passing due to heart failure in 1977, she enjoyed a Fannie Lou Hamer Day in Ruleville and saw *Mississippi* magazine name her as one of Mississippi's six greatest "Women of Influence." Her death was noted by everyone from Stokely Carmichael to the *New York Times,* and, most significantly, the 1977 Mississippi House of Representatives voted 116-0 to praise her for a lifetime of devotion to equality and justice and for serving as a "symbol to people across the nation in their struggle for human dignity."

JOURNALISTIC INTEGRITY, BY DAMN

When ex-University of Alabama sorority beauty queen Hazel Brannon Smith drove her Cadillac convertible across the Big Black River bridge into the sleepy town of Durant in 1935, no one expected the ultraconservative girl in the designer dress, spiked heels, and wide-brimmed Hattie Carnegie hat to cause much political furor. Even after she purchased the *Durant News* that year, and the *Lexington Advertiser* seven years later, no one had any inkling of the extraordinary controversy soon to come. The only eyebrows raised by this dyed-in-the-wool Dixiecrat, defender of Joe McCarthy, and opponent of both communism and integration were those of starry-eyed, wishful-thinking suitors. Indeed, Smith seemed initially content to fill her *Through Hazel Eyes* column with diatribes against bootleggers and bullying sheriffs, once criticizing a sheriff involved in Holmes County's illegal liquor racket by calling him a liar with "no more remorse than an egg-sucking dog."

That soon changed when she interviewed the widow of a black man who had been whipped to death by local racist thugs. Although a judge gave her a suspended jail sentence and fined her fifty dollars for publishing the statements of an eyewitness (the widow) during a pending murder trial, she ultimately got his decision reversed by the Mississippi Supreme Court. Her conversion to the cause of social justice became complete when, in 1954, she ran a story accusing Holmes County sheriff Richard Byrd of shooting a fleeing black man in the back. In it, she pointed out that America's laws are for everyone, and most local residents do not condone abusing black people. "Byrd has violated every concept of justice, decency and right. He is not fit to occupy office," she wrote.

Byrd promptly filed a libel lawsuit and was awarded a $10,000 judgment, which was also reversed by the state's highest court. But Smith's newspapers began losing revenues, a cross was burned on her lawn, and her editorial offices were firebombed. Subsequently viewed by many Holmes Countians as a "velvet-covered thorn," Smith nevertheless joined fellow journalists Ira Harkey of Pascagoula and Oliver Emmerich of McComb in waging an all-out war against local racial injustice and in support of freedom of the press. When Byrd later threatened a black man for publicly condemning racist local politics, Smith refused to let the matter drop and penned a column saying that Byrd's job was to enforce the law not make it. "He will have a full time job if he does that," she fumed. Smith boldly declared that she would oppose any attempt by the sheriff to limit freedom of the press. "When free citizens are afraid to speak," she concluded, "then dictatorship ceases to be a printed word and becomes an ugly reality."

Upon familiarizing himself with the Smith-Byrd controversy, a visiting *New York Post* reporter said that it would take a braver man than himself to look the sheriff in the eye again, "but praise God, it takes a braver man than the sheriff to look Hazel in the eye."

Smith continued her campaign for racial justice into the next decade, writing in 1962 that Mississippi had more to fear from the homegrown fascism of the white Citizens' Councils than from communism. "Worrying unduly about the so-called 'communist menace' in Mississippi," she wrote, "is something like a minister orating on the sins of the people in Timbuktu when his own congregation sits uneasily on skid row."

Although Smith received the 1964 Pulitzer Prize for her efforts, the seventies ushered in an era in which blacks no longer needed her support, and she remained too defiant to be accepted back into the good graces of the local white society. And when, in 1982, her husband fell off the roof of their under-construction mansion, an updated version of *Gone with the Wind*'s Tara, she never again enjoyed the same zest for life that had carried her through her greatest difficulties. Her fall from grace was complete three years later when the *Advertiser* folded under $200,000 debt. She died in Alabama in 1989 of complications of Alzheimer's and liver cancer, but not before establishing herself as another of the river country's bravest souls, and forever raising the bar for all would-be muckraking journalists.

TURNABOUT IS FAIR PLAY

From 1890 to 1970, racist, archconservative politicians held on to river-country political power by whatever means they could, including brute force by the KKK, racist demagoguery in state politics, unconstitutional local measures such as the poll tax, and numerous other brands of political chicanery. One of the favorite tricks of crooked politicians was "ballot stuffing," accomplished by sending a worker into a voting booth to steal an official blank ballot, replace it with a blank piece of paper, and slip out with the real ballot in his pocket. The ballot was then filled out with a candidate's name and another voter paid to cast that ballot and return with another blank ballot, and so on ad nauseam.

Another tried and true method involved the "sample ballot." After paying off community leaders for permission to do so, a candidate would have his workers hand out sample ballots in the "bought" community with a check beside his name so the people would know to cast their votes for him. After enduring such shenanigans for years, the honest politicians began devising means to outwit and discombobulate the racist crooks at their own infernal games.

One such situation occurred in the mid-1970s when a progressive Delta politician opposed a crafty, longtime incumbent for an important county office. Upon discovering that the incumbent had "greased a few palms" in a community and had printed up thousands of sample ballots for distribution in several area neighborhoods, the progressive's supporters cut a deal with the local printer to substitute the progressive's sample ballots for the incumbent's. The day after his defeat, the incumbent discovered the means by which he had been vanquished. When he accosted the progressive and accused him of violating election laws, his opponent replied with a grin, "Printing fake ballots is not a crime. Distributing them is. It was your men, not mine, who distributed those sample ballots. Nevertheless, since your help proved so valuable to my campaign, I've decided not to press charges against you!"

In the sixties and seventies, the Delta elected its first black legislators since Reconstruction, including Ebenezer's Robert Clark and Clarksdale's Aaron Henry. White moderates William Winter and Evelyn Gandy took the governorship and lieutenant governorship, respectively, and progressive white Delta legislators such as Greenville's Howard Dyer and Greenwood's John Fraiser joined with Clark and Henry to wrest legislative control away from the Closed Society archconservatives. Whether by moral hook or by ironic, electoral crook, the Revolt of the Rednecks had finally been laid to rest, and Mississippi river-country politics was, after over a half-century's lapse, free to resume its place in the American political mainstream.

THE BOY WHO BECAME A FROG

T. Kermit Scott grew up in the 1940s in pulchritudinous Leland, Mississippi, eight miles due east of Greenville. Once known as the "Hellhole of the Delta" for its abundance of turn-of-the century blind-tiger saloons, Leland ultimately became one the Delta's loveliest small towns with its wide streets, stately homes, and ancient oak and cypress trees. Leland's most beautiful attraction has always been Deer Creek, which winds lazily through the heart of town. Since 1961, Lelanders have presented the now-famous Floating Christmas Parade, in which Santa and other waterborne seasonal floats are stationed in the creek.

It was on Deer Creek's banks in the 1940s that ten-year-old Kermit Scott and his best friend, Jim, went on their boyhood expeditions foraging for turtles, tadpoles, and bullfrogs. After high school, Kermit and Jim parted ways and set out to make their fortunes away from the river country. In time, the boyhood pals fell completely out of touch.

Deer Creek, Leland

Many years later, while a philosophy professor at Purdue University, Kermit read a 1979 *New York Times Magazine* article in which his now-famous friend, Jim Henson, revealed that he had named his popular Muppet creation, Kermit the Frog, after the childhood pal with whom he had explored Deer Creek's banks!

The Birthplace of the Frog, a museum honoring the late "Sesame Street" hero Jim Henson, now graces the same creek bank upon which Jim and Kermit once frolicked. Museum visitors discover original Muppet memorabilia, including a prominent display that tells the unusual and delightful tale of the Boy Who Became a Frog.

WHAT, ME WORRY?

The riverboat gambler's spirit still runs deep in the Mississippi river country. For example, mid-1990s Ole Miss head football coach Tommy Tuberville so frequently confounded opponents by faking Rebel punts, calling for two-point conversions in the fourth quarter of crucial SEC games, and "going for it" on fourth down that the national media dubbed him Mississippi's "riverboat gambler." In much the same spirit, Mississippi attorney general Mike Moore gambled his political career on an unprecedented 1996 David vs. Goliath assault on the tobacco industry, which ultimately brought billionaire tobacco magnates to their knees and a $200 million payoff to the state of Mississippi. But perhaps the greatest modern-day river-country gambler of them all is ex-Louisiana governor Edwin

Edwards, the "high-rolling charmer" who survived over two dozen public scandals and investigations until a stunning extortion conviction in 2000.

Edwards' flamboyant gamesmanship surfaced in his comments as the federal government geared up to prosecute that extortion charge. Indicted in 1998 for allegedly extorting millions in payoffs to steer riverboat casino licenses to friends and cronies while governor, Edwards declared, "It's less than I expected. I'm not charged with the Oklahoma City bombing." When informed that the charges carried a maximum sentence of 350 years and a $7.5 million fine, Edwards deadpanned, "I can truthfully say if my sentence is 350 years, I don't plan to serve."

CANADIAN CLUB

Although football is many a Southerner's second religion, baseball remains the national pastime, and the game that Babe Ruth and Mark McGwire saved has always known its share of devotees in the Mississippi river country. The old Cotton States League thrived during the 1940s and 1950s in Natchez, Greenville, Clarksdale, and Greenwood, giving birth to rivalries as heated as any in the major leagues. The Greenwood Dodgers were a Brooklyn Dodgers farm club, and lucky youngsters chosen as batboys-for-the-day rubbed shoulders with future stars like Eddie Stanky and Walter Alston. In Memphis, Jackson, and New Orleans, Starkville's Cool Papa Bell thrilled local Negro League fans with his blazing speed and derring-do on the base paths.

Ole Miss vs. State, Jackson

And one river-country homeboy, Greenwood's Clay Hopper, played a major role in baseball's (and possibly America's) greatest societal experiment of the 1940s. In 1946, Dodger owner Branch Rickey introduced Jackie Robinson as the first black player for the Dodgers' Montreal farm club. When Hopper, the Royals' manager, saw Robinson for the first time, he declared,"Well, when Mr. Rickey picked one, he sure picked a black one."

Initially opposed to Robinson's presence on grounds that he (Hopper) would be vilified in the South for supporting baseball's integration, Hopper once responded to Rickey's comment that Robinson was "superhuman" by asking the owner if he really believed Robinson was actually a human being. Rickey promptly informed Hopper that he would not only manage Robinson but would manage him in the manner that Rickey intended, making full use of the new star's extraordinary talents.

Thusly admonished, Hopper quickly warmed to the task, aiding Robinson's transition from shortstop to second base, and inserting a squeeze play into the Royals' game plan which put Robby's superb base-running skills on national display. When the season ended, Hopper, a changed man and firm believer in Jackie Robinson, told the future Hall of Famer, "You're a great ballplayer and a fine gentleman. It's been wonderful having you on the team." Hopper also reported to Rickey, "You don't have to worry none about [Robinson]. He's the greatest competitor I ever saw, and what's more, he's a gentleman."

Hopper's biggest test came a few years later when Robinson and the fully integrated Dodgers came to Greenwood during a postseason barnstorming tour. According to black Brooklyn pitcher Don Newcombe, who, along with Roy Campanella, had recently followed in Robinson's footsteps, Hopper risked his reputation in Greenwood by unabashedly shaking hands with the Dodgers' black players, much to the chagrin of the "out and out racists" in attendance. Newcombe told author Peter Golenbock that Hopper was a fair-minded, courageous man who never made racist remarks and who stood by his team despite criticism from Southern racists.

Thanks in small part to Hopper's willingness to change and his timely mentoring of young black players like Robinson, Newcombe, and Campanella, baseball rose to unprecedented heights in the 1950s as America's favorite sport, and a nation took its first twentieth-century steps towards becoming a land of opportunity and freedom for all.

MISSISSIPPI MULES PACK A HECKUVA WALLOP

From 1959 to 1963, Johnny Vaught's Ole Miss Rebels laid claim to the title of America's premier college football team and, from 1947 to 1973, were easily one of the nation's top five programs, winning three national championships and six SEC titles, attending a record fifteen straight bowls, producing twenty-seven All-Americans, and having their 1959 squad selected as the SEC Team of the Decade and the third greatest team of all time. But by the late 1960s the Rebels had fallen off several notches and were even being challenged for Mississippi supremacy by their cross-state rival, Mississippi State. Onto this stage stepped Archie Manning, a thin, lightly recruited, freckle-faced, red-haired kid from the river-country town of Drew. After Manning directed several last-minute come-from-behind victories during his sophomore season, the media dubbed him "The Mississippi Rifle" and touted the Rebels as preseason favorites to take the 1969 SEC crown.

Standing in their way was the SEC's newest titan, the Tennessee Volunteers, led by their All-American linebacker, Steve Kiner. When asked by a reporter during the 1969 preseason if he thought Mississippi had the horses, Kiner, whose team had shellacked Manning's Rebels the previous year 31-0, replied that he thought the Rebels were a "bunch of mules."

"But what about Archie?" a stunned scribe inquired.

"Archie who?" Kiner asked.

John Vaught promptly placed that newspaper article on the Rebels' bulletin board, and when the teams met in Jackson that fall for a much-publicized showdown, Manning and his "Mules" crushed the Big Orange 38-0. As a direct result of the upset, the Sugar Bowl bypassed Tennessee and extended its New Year's Day bid to Ole Miss. The Rebels whipped Arkansas in New Orleans and finished the '69 season ranked eighth in the nation. A song soon hit the airwaves entitled "The Ballad of Archie Who," which expressed the sentiments of most Mississippians—"Archie ('Super') Manning should run for president!"

Manning garnered All-America honors at Ole Miss and was later voted the NFC's Most Valuable Player while quarterbacking the hapless New Orleans Saints. His son Eli, a Prep All-American quarterback, will soon be directing the resurgent Rebel attack and will, along with new Ole Miss head coach David Cutcliff, surely return the Red and Blue to its glory days of old! And with Mississippi State recently dumping its perennial SEC doormat status by becoming 1998 Co-Champion of the SEC West Division, the Egg Bowl, now covered by national television on Thanksgiving nights, may yet become the brightest jewel in King Football's glorious crown.

WILDCATS, TIGERS, AND BEARS—OH YES!

The Mississippi river country has produced more than its share of extraordinary athletes, including baseballers Dizzy Dean, Will Clark, George Scott, Hugh Critz, Rafael Palmeiro, Boo Ferriss, Donnie Kessinger, Jeff Brantly, Ellis Burkes, Lenny Dykstra, Bobby Thigpen, Jeff Fassero, David Delucci, Carlton Loewer, and Dave Parker; basketballers Jeff Malone, Bailey Howell, Clarence Witherspoon, Johnny Newman, John Stroud, Purvis Short, Lindsey Hunter, Nick Revon, Erick Dampier, Gerald Glass, Ansu Sesay, Wiley Peck, Keith Carter, and Tyrone Washington; Olympians Willey B. White, Roy Cochran, Ruthie Bolton, and Calvin Smith; and golfers Cary Middlecoff, Jim Gallagher, Jr., and Glen Day.

But it's the football stars who make the Deep South's world go round, and the river country has produced more than its share of gridiron greats, including Archie Manning, Brett Favre, Jerry Rice, Charlie Connerly, Jake Gibbs, Lance Alworth, Ray Guy, Jackie Parker,

Steve McNair, D. D. Lewis, L. C. Greenwood, Lem Barney, Hugh Green, David ("Deacon") Jones, Frank ("Bruiser") Kinard, Parker Hall, Wilbert Montgomery, Leon Lett, Sammy Winder, Eric Moulds, Kent Hull, John Avery, J. J. Johnson, Rufus French, Reggie Collier, Willie Green, Marcus Dupree, Deuce McAllister, Patrick Surtain, Ben Williams, Tony Bennet, Jeff Herod, Kent Austin, John Fourcade, Frank Dowsing, Wesley Walls, Barney Poole, Tim Bowens, Rocky Felker, Billy Brewer, Freddie Joe Nunn, Willie Totten, Glynn Griffin, Doug Cunningham, Stan Hindman, Wayne Harris, Bill Stacy, Mardye McDole, Romaro Miller, Jim Dunaway, Showboat Boykin, Johnnie Cooks, Larry Grantham, Harper Davis, Ed ("Goat") Hale, Fred Smoot, songwriter Jimmy Weatherly, comedian Jerry Clower, and perhaps the greatest ballplayer of them all—Walter ("Sweetness") Payton.

A star running back for the Jackson State Tigers, Payton scored an NCAA career record 464 points and then became the NFL's most prolific rusher, amassing a record 16,726 yards and 110 rushing touchdowns during a thirteen-year pro career. He led his Chicago Bears to a resounding victory in Super Bowl XX and was recently inducted in the Pro Football Hall of Fame. But while many football fans are familiar with Payton's college and pro football feats, they may not be aware of his career-launching first play for his high-school team, the Columbia Wildcats.

Nestled on the Pearl River's banks, tiny Columbia, Mississippi, has achieved fame for producing the world's best barbecued ribs and the NFL's greatest rusher. But in 1970, Payton's place had two racially separate high schools, one of which was the all-black John Jefferson High School. Walter very nearly didn't play football there at all, preferring instead to play in the school band. And although he really didn't care to follow in the football footsteps of his standout brother Eddie, once Eddie graduated, Walter became Jefferson High's newest football hero. Along the way, he acquired the nickname "Spiderman," for his uncanny ability to climb walls and leap fences in a single bound.

When, in 1971, high-school integration came to the Mississippi river country, Payton transferred to the previously all white Columbia High School for his senior year. With many college scouts in attendance, Payton took his first handoff on the initial play of his first integrated game. He made the most of the opportunity, running off tackle for eighty yards, the last fifteen backwards, and scoring on that very first play! But the scouts from all the mostly white SEC schools wrote Payton off as hot dog because of his flashy run, and foolishly failed to extend him a scholarship. But Jackson State University recognized Payton's potential and later discovered what everyone in Columbia already knew, that "Sweetness" was anything but a self-centered hot dog. Walter Payton proved to be the most unselfish, modest, and disciplined player the game would ever know, and the rest, as they say, was pro-football history.

And he, too, inspired a song, "The Ballad of Walter Payton," which leaves no doubt about "who's the fastest man around."

ART ON THE HALF-SHELL

The Mississippi river country has also produced and nurtured a wealth of artistic talent, including primitivist and rural-life painter Theora Hamblett, renowned landscape and abstract portraitist Marie Hull, impressionist Dick Kelso, folk artists Alice Moseley and M. B. Mayfield, watercolor virtuosos Walter Anderson and Wyatt Waters, and revolutionary abstract potter George Ohr, a.k.a. the "Mad Potter of Biloxi." Many of these artists' works were shared with the world by artists' colonies such as John and Hosford Fontaine's Allison's Wells, the Anderson family's Shearwater Pottery, and the Mississippi Art Colony.

But perhaps the greatest river-country artist was Ocean Springs' Walter Anderson, who lived his art as few masters ever do. Anderson's studio was Horn Island, located in the Mississippi Sound ten miles due south of where the Pascagoula River empties into the Gulf of Mexico. Virtually unknown during his lifetime, Anderson's primitive wildlife watercolor portraits have recently garnered national acclaim. They were made all the more interesting by the discovery of his diary, in which Anderson recorded his exploits on the island from 1944 to his death in 1965. These writings reveal how the already reclusive Anderson, once described as "a Robinson Crusoe with the inclinations of St. Francis," shut himself off from the world to revel in nature's beauty and immortalize her subjects on his island-based Garden of Eden.

More importantly, these entries yield marvelous insights into both the artist's viewpoint and mission in life. Describing a lovely midsummer's evening, Anderson gave a hint of his vision of the world when he wrote:

> Last night there was a beautiful sunset. One felt that it had been arranged with taste. So many sunsets seem simply to be wild expositions of color in order to stun people into a state of mute wonder. But this one had variety, vermilion red and purple together, and lilac and gold together against a heavenly clear green turquoise sky. You felt that there would never be bad weather again.

But Anderson did more than observe. In order to satisfy his Muse, he endured a life-threatening hurricane, ate nothing except what he took from the island and the sea, used his hat to trap snakes and birds for painting, and waded lagoons to get better views of alligators, pelicans, oysters, crabs, and rare flora. Anderson the sojourner ultimately became as much a native of Horn Island as any of its other inhabitants, thereby allowing Anderson the artist to more fully realize his artistic destiny whenever he stumbled upon a classic subject, in one case, a creature with "two bright yellow eyes, one on each side of an elevated beak, with honey colored stripes leading down from them and incredible feet grasping with unnecessary competence the dead bullrushes. 'Ha,' said I, 'this is Moses, and I am the Egyptian princess come to take him back to a royal world.' So I did a watercolor of Moses when I got back to camp."

THE CUP THAT CHEERS AND A SPEAKER WITH NO PEERS

Deep South folks have always experienced a love-hate relationship with liquor—they love to imbibe but hate to publicly admit it. In Alabama, this once took the form of a ban on all restaurant- and nightclub-served liquor except that sold in miniature bottles. In South Louisiana, the only laws proscribing hooch are those established by the federal government, and those prevail only as long as the time it takes Louisianans to figure out a lawful way to circumvent them. But in Mississippi, "dry" counties still exist next to "wet" ones, and no less booze is consumed in the former than in the latter. Of course, this is the state where, during Prohibition, the government collected a tax on *illegal bootleg whisky!* It's also the place where William F. Winter, now famous as one of Mississippi's first racially moderate governors, once garnered great wealth as the official collector of the state's illegal-liquor tax, then successfully campaigned for another political office on the basis of having subsequently done away with the liquor tax collection system!

But Mississippi's greatest moment during the prohibition debate came in the form of a 1952 speech by state legislator N. S. ("Soggy") Sweat, Jr., a prominent Corinth lawyer and much-loved Ole Miss law-school professor. Made at a time when Mississippi was a completely "dry" state that collected a profitable illegal-liquor tax, Sweat's Whisky Speech remains a time-honored classic:

> My friends, I had not intended to discuss this controversial subject at this particular time. However, I want you to know that I do not shun controversy. On the contrary, I will take a stand on any issue at any time, regardless of how fraught with controversy it might be. You have asked me how I feel about whisky. All right, here is how I feel about whisky. . . .
>
> If when you say whisky you mean the devil's brew, the poison scourge, the bloody monster, that defiles innocence, dethrones reason, destroys the home, creates misery and poverty, yea, literally takes the bread from mouths of little children; if you mean the evil drink that topples the Christian man and woman from the pinnacle of righteousness, gracious living into the bottomless pit of degradation, and despair, and shame and helplessness, and hopelessness, then certainly I am against it.
>
> But, if when you say whisky you mean the oil of conversation, the philosophic wine, the ale that is consumed when good fellows get together, that puts a song in their hearts and laughter on their lips, and the warm glow of contentment in their eyes; if you mean Christmas cheer; if you mean the stimulating drink that puts the spring in the old gentleman's step on a frosty, crispy morning; if you mean the drink which enables a man to magnify his joy, and his happiness, and to forget, if only for a little while, life's great tragedies, and heartaches and sorrows; if you mean that drink, the sale of which pours into our treasuries untold millions of dollars, which are used to provide tender care for our little crippled children, our blind, our deaf, our dumb, our pitiful aged and infirm; to build highways and hospitals and schools, then certainly I am for it.
>
> *This is my stand. I will not retreat from it. I will not compromise.*

RIVER EATS

The Mississippi river country is home to many great restaurants, and not all of them are of the pretentious yet vanilla "fine dining" variety that serve raw fish and baked buffalo livers to anxious, middle-aged, suburban patrons. Some are unique in all the world, often combining world-class food with out-of-this-world atmosphere.

Natchez's King's Tavern Restaurant serves some of the best prime rib and barbecued shrimp on the Mississippi River, but guests must expect to brave a few otherworldly incidents during their evening's repast. Constructed of brick and flatboat's timbers by the British around 1760, the three-story building's bullet-ridden door and barred windows suggest that it may have initially served as a blockhouse on the old Trace. Before being converted to a restaurant in 1798, it also served as a principal mail and stagecoach station on that infamous roadway. A bear's and a cougar's claw prints decorate the present-day restaurant's floor, but they are hardly the main attraction.

King's Tavern is haunted by Madeline, a serving girl and mistress to Prosper King, the tavern's original owner. She mysteriously disappeared, but a 1930s discovery of three skeletons in the restaurant's walls and a jewel-encrusted Spanish knife in the chimney lent support to the long-held theory that King's jealous wife murdered Madeline. The other skeletons are believed to belong to a young girl and a Natchez Indian chief who were also murdered on the restaurant's grounds.

The tavern's patrons frequently experience lights switching on and off by themselves, hear footsteps on the empty third floor, find puddles of water in places where no water

King's Tavern Restaurant, Natchez

could have been, and hear pots and pans rattling by themselves. The wait staff occasionally suffers ghostly pranks such as being tripped by closing doors, bombed by falling glasses, and clunked by suddenly opening cabinet doors. Most impressive of all, the dumbwaiter occasionally operates itself. These events may be caused by the ghosts of the murdered girl and Indian chief, the latter occasionally materializing wearing his feather-laden war bonnet. More than likely these manifestations are caused by Madeline herself as she vainly searches for her long-lost love or expresses disdain for a new owner, waiter, or customer. Either way, King's Tavern offers one of the river country's most unusual dining experiences.

Way down upon the Yazoo River, Greenwood's Lusco's Restaurant is the favorite of Delta diners. It was built during 1930s Prohibition by Charles Lusco, who realized that no law could prevent Deltonians from imbibing, and wild horses couldn't keep the local gentry away from good food. Located in a dive quite literally "across the tracks" from

Lusco's Restaurant, Greenwood

downtown, Lusco's offers divinely prepared steak, seafood, chicken, and pasta, always at the Delta's most reasonable prices. Patrons may be served behind drawn curtains in private rooms where the touch of a buzzer brings white-coated waiters a'calling. The private rooms were originally devised for Prohibition drinkers who wished to sample Lusco's moonshine and homemade beer.

Nowadays, Lusco's customers may dine near the jukebox when in a musical mood or bring their own alcoholic refreshment to satisfy special libation fancies. And although the waiters no longer sing the menu to patrons, and guests are no longer allowed to fling butter pats up to the ceiling or walk atop the partitions between the private booths, the quality of food and service hasn't diminished while four more generations of Luscos have acquired and run the restaurant.

They serve Mississippi's best lunch just across the downtown tracks from Lusco's at Greenwood's Crystal Grill, another Prohibition-era hotspot-turned-family restaurant. Although this place once earned notoriety when, as the Crystal Club, it only served whites, current owner Johnny Ballas makes everybody feel welcome, whether dining in booths in the older, forward section or at tables in the plush new back rooms. There, patrons decide between delicious fresh seafood, several tasty pasta dishes, unbeatable fried chicken, topnotch steaks, healthy vegetables, delectable homemade pies, and much, much more. But many go for the breaded veal cutlets, the annual favorite of Crystal customers statewide.

Westward down Highway 82 in the Mississippi River city of Greenville is Doe's Eat Place, which serves the largest and most delicious steaks in Mississippi, as well as some unbeatable, spicy hot tamales. Housed since 1941 in a dilapidated old building, Doe's serves its gigantic steaks (the smallest weighs two pounds) in one of two small rooms or in the kitchen, and always on rickety old tables. After dining on the Southland's best beef, customers may head up the street for authentic down-home rhythm and blues entertainment.

In upper Pearl River country, Peggy's Restaurant is a favorite of Philadelphia's folks. At Peggy's, customers help themselves to an all-they-can-eat lunch buffet of fried chicken, pork chops, and other finger-licking-good Southern delicacies. "Help themselves" is the key phrase, because owner Peggy Webb supplies no "hired help." Patrons dine on the honor system—eating their fill and then leaving cash payment in the basket by the front door on their way out! There are no waiters, no register, and no problem, at least not where Peggy's is concerned.

One of eastern Mississippi's best surf-and-turf restaurants is the Tombigbee River country's pride, Weidmann's Restaurant. Begun in 1870 as Swiss immigrant Felix Weidmann's fruit and vegetable stand, the enterprise soon grew from four stools and a counter to a large, European-style eatery with beer steins and deer heads decorating its walls. For the customer interested in experiencing a taste of the good old days, Weidmann's serves a delicious black-bottom pie in the "1870 Room."

Anyone preferring a mobile lunch may head to the central Mississippi town of Mendenhall, where he or she will discover the pride of the Strong River country's eateries, The Revolving Table Restaurant. Chicken and dumplings, mashed and sweet potatoes, greens, gobs of gravy, cornbread, and homemade pies are among the traditional Southern treats guaranteed to turn diners' heads as the dishes spin by on the lazy Susan. "Eat till it ouches" is the house motto, and no one has ever known whether this refers to the pain of overeating or the wear and tear on elbows and wrists from spinning the lazy Susan for seconds, thirds, and fourths.

Housed in one of Biloxi's oldest buildings, Mary Mahoney's Old French House serves the best French cuisine on the Mississippi Coast. Constructed in 1737, the Old French House is graced by the presence within its brick-walled courtyard of the towering Patriarch Oak, believed to be over two thousand years old. This place exudes Old World atmosphere, offering several elegant dining rooms in the main house, open-air dining in the courtyard, and a lounge in the building's old slave quarters, as well as a more casual European-style

Mary Mahoney's Old French House, Biloxi

Soul-food restaurant, Greenwood

sidewalk café. There is also the original brick-walled wine cellar, wide random-width board floors, handmade-brick walls, hand-hewn cypress columns, and a roof made of French-imported slate. Suffice it to say, Bienville would have been proud to say he had dined at the French House, and for all we know, he may very well have done so.

These and other fine river-country establishments will continue to serve the best food in the most unique environs to be found between Memphis and New Orleans, at least until the hurricane blows or the rivers overflow their banks!

THE GIRL THE MISSISSIPPI RIVER COULDN'T BEAT

Variously known by river-country inhabitants as Father of Waters, Great Waters, Old-Big-Strong, Old Man, and Ole Miss, the Mississippi River has always engendered feelings of both love and (during flood season) fear. River-country businessman and writer David Cohn once described the Mississippi River as a "wild and primitive force, the abode of a river god often malevolent and always inscrutable." Novelist William Faulkner, who created a river of his own, the Yoknapatawpha, likened the Mississippi's destructive penchant for overflowing its banks to a mule's personality: "As a mule, will work for you ten years for the privilege of kicking you once." Greenvillian William Alexander Percy once described the river as a "shifting, unappeasable god." But it was Delta blacks residing near its banks who most eloquently described the river's "ownwayishness," saying that the river was "high handed when she took a notion," and sorrowfully acknowledging, "Ole

Miss always took her part—the fattest calf, a strip of the blackest land, a child or even a man. Yes, this land belong to Ole Miss, and Ole Miss was bound to get her share."

Indeed, the river has always taken its share, for just as the Father of Waters gave the river country the world's most fertile cotton-farming land, so too has it made ghost towns of many once-prosperous communities by unexpectedly changing its course or eroding the ground right out from under them. In 1848, the river completely rerouted itself in Tunica County, leaving county seat Port Royal high and dry. Then, after the folks established a new county seat in a town appropriately named Delta, the river reclaimed the land around that village in 1890 and it slid beneath the Mississippi's surface. The river abandoned the prosperous cotton town Rodney in 1869 and later devoured fifty-five city blocks of nearby Grand Gulf, ultimately consigning both towns to oblivion.

But the Father of Waters has always been too democratic with its children to simply wipe out a few towns situated on its banks. It frequently breaches its banks and floods millions of acres at a time, spreading death, destruction, and disease among a helpless, terrorized populace. Between 1858 and 1922, eleven major floods ravaged the Mississippi Delta, but the worst Mississippi river-country disaster of all time was occasioned by the notorious Great Flood of 1927. On April 21 of that year, the levee burst at Scott, Mississippi, a village 18 miles north of Greenville, sending water into the Delta flatlands at a rate of 468,000 cubic feet per second. Traveling at speeds of up to 14 miles per hour, producing a sound likened to "a thousand freight trains," the floodwaters laid waste to everything in their path. Over 16.5 million Mississippi acres (2.7 million acres of farmland) and 162,000 homes languished under from five to twenty feet of water for twelve terrible weeks. In Mississippi alone, over 42,000 homes, 21,000 other buildings, and 10,200 privies were destroyed; over 40,000 horses, mules, cattle, and hogs were killed; and over 500 human lives were lost. The cost of the flooding of an area 30 miles wide and 100 miles long was estimated at $200 million. In Louisiana, 1.3 million acres of farmland were inundated and 700,000 people were rendered homeless.

But these are just statistics, and the effect of the '27 flood upon the populace defied mere statistical measurement. Alligator gar five feet long, deadly water moccasins as thick as a man's thigh, two-foot-long rats, and rampaging seven-foot-long alligators took up residence in people's homes, deep wells, and backyards. The mud, filth, and stench were unbearable, especially during 1927's unusually hot summer. To make matters worse, malaria, typhoid fever, dysentery, pellagra, and polio ravaged an already disease-ridden Delta populace unaware of the latest means of prevention and lacking the medical resources to carry them out.

Worst of all, many survivors of the tidal wave were left stranded for days on rooftops and levees. In *Father Mississippi,* Lyle Saxon described a tragic scene near the river town of Greenville where survivors, black and white, wealthy and poor, huddled together on levee tops, without food or water, "afraid to sleep, too miserable to cry."

Old Levee Board Building (1883),
Mississippi River levee, Greenville

When Leland lawyer and farmer Eugene Gerald saw the floodwaters approaching his hometown on the morning of April 23, he put his wife, May, their eight-year-old daughter, Martha, and her younger siblings, Gene and Lucy, on a train bound for Iuka. When his family returned to Leland three months later, Eugene allowed his two older children to accompany him in his twelve-foot johnboat as he rowed across the county to aid their friends and neighbors. Unaware of the dangers represented by potentially disease ridden floodwaters, Martha and Gene contracted polio during one of their trips. The disease proved fatal to Gene and also came close to claiming Martha's life. Placed in a body cast for six months, she survived the infection, but not before succumbing to the disease's terrible crippling effects.

The family struggled mightily to overcome these unhappy circumstances, and the arrival of another baby girl, Adelyn, greatly lifted their spirits. But shortly after her birth, the Great Depression swept through the Delta with a vengeance and, in concert with the ubiquitous boll weevil, added poverty to the list of woes suffered by river-country denizens.

Steeled by years of physical pain and economic hardship, but buoyed by the supportive ties of a loving family and close-knit community, young Martha did well in school, ultimately graduating cum laude from Millsaps College in 1941. Not wishing to be pigeonholed into the then-traditional women's careers of teacher or secretary, Martha followed in her father's footsteps and entered the University of Mississippi Law School, one of only three women to do so that year. Initially ignored by her male classmates, Martha nevertheless became editor in chief of the law journal and graduated with honors in 1944.

Even after she had become the senior partner of one of Jackson's largest law firms in 1977, and had made the prestigious listing of *The Best Lawyers in America* in 1991, Martha never forgot the difficulties she had faced in her youth and did her part to help those less fortunate than herself. She offered her support, gifts, and leadership to the local colleges, the arts community, the YWCA, the United Methodist Missions, and the Central Mississippi Legal Services. While championing women's rights in the 1980s, she answered a politician's assertion that his political party "placed women on a pedestal" by saying, "Women can't make a living on a pedestal."

As former lieutenant governor Evelyn Gandy said of her in 1997 upon her death at age seventy-eight, "Martha was a guiding light for many Mississippi women professionals who followed her." Shortly before her passing, a young lawyer asked her opinion as to the most important quality a lawyer should possess besides competence. "Integrity," she replied without hesitation, "and remember that no one can be a little dishonest any more than they could be a little pregnant. The accident of your birth ensured that you'd never be pregnant," she added, with a familiar, mirthful glint in her eye. "Now you can make certain that you're never dishonest."

Integrity, courage, resilience, compassion, and tenacity—these are the qualities that, to paraphrase Mr. Faulkner, have always allowed the river-country people to not only endure, but to prevail. It should therefore come as no surprise that these character traits were to be found in abundance in Martha Gerald, the Girl the Mississippi River Couldn't Beat.

SELECTED BIBLIOGRAPHY

The author's two favorite research sources were the oral histories found at the Mississippi Department of Archives and History and numerous articles in the *Journal of Mississippi History,* also produced by the Department of Archives. This is a partial list of other books the author relied upon or quoted during the completion of *Mississippi River Country Tales.*

Asbury, Herbert. *The French Quarter.* New York: Pocket Books, 1981.

Baker, Lewis. *The Percys of Mississippi: Politics and Literature in the New South.* Baton Rouge: Louisiana State University Press, 1983.

Baldwin, Joseph G. *The Flush Times of Mississippi and Alabama.* Baton Rouge: Louisiana State University Press, 1987.

Botkin, B. A. *A Treasury of Mississippi River Folklore.* Prineville, Ore.: Bonanza Books, 1978.

Brieger, James F. *Hometown Mississippi.* 1980.

Cain, Cyril E. *Four Centuries on the Pascagoula.* 1984.

Claiborne, J. F. H. *Mississippi as a Province, Territory and State.* Jackson: Mississippi Department of Archives and History, 1880.

Coats, Robert. *The Outlaw Years.* Lincoln: University of Nebraska Press, 1986.

Cobb, James C. *The Mississippi Delta and the World: The Memoirs of David C. Cohn.* Baton Rouge: Louisiana State University Press, 1995.

———. *The Most Southern Place on Earth.* New York: Oxford University Press, 1992.

Cox, James L. *Mississippi Almanac 1997-98: The Ultimate Reference on the State.* 1997.

Crocker, Mary Wallace. *Historic Architecture in Mississippi.* Jackson: University Press of Mississippi, 1973.

Daniels, Jonathan. *The Devil's Backbone: The Story of the Natchez Trace.* Gretna, La.: Pelican Publishing Company, 1985.

Davis, Burke. *The Civil War: Strange & Fascinating Facts.* Catasauqua, Pa.: Fairfax Press, 1982.

Dunbar, Rowland. *A History of Mississippi: The Heart of the South.* 1978.

Faulkner, William. *Requiem for a Nun.* New York: Random House, 1975.

Foote, Shelby Foote. *Shiloh.* New York: Vintage Books, 1991.

Fraiser, Jim. *M Is for Mississippi: An Irreverent Guide to the Magnolia State.* Jackson, Miss.: Persimmon Press, 1993.

Golenbock, Peter. *Bums: An Oral History of the Brooklyn Dodgers.* New York: G. P. Putnam's Sons, 1984.

Green, R., ed. *Journal of Chickasaw History,* vol. 2. 1996.

Hammons, Ann R. *Wild Bill Sullivan: King of the Hollow.* Jackson: University Press of Mississippi, 1980.

Hogan, William R. *William Johnson's Natchez.* Baton Rouge: Louisiana State University Press, 1951.

Holmes, William F. *The White Chief James Kimble Vardaman.* Baton Rouge: Louisiana State University Press, 1970.

Huber, Leonard. *New Orleans: A Pictoral History* Gretna, La.: Pelican Publishing Company, 1991.

——. *Tales of the Mississippi.* Gretna, La.: Pelican Publishing Company, 1981.

Hurst, Jack. *Nathan Bedford Forrest: A Biography.* New York: Vintage Books, 1993.

Karl, Frederick R. *William Faulkner: American Writer.* North Pomfret, Vt.: Weidenfield & Nicolson, 1989.

Leavitt, Mel. *A Short History of New Orleans.* San Francisco: Lexicos, 1982.

Loewen, James W. *Mississippi: Conflict and Change.* New York: Random House, 1974.

Lowry, Robert. *A History of Mississippi.* 1978.

Lyttle, Andrew. *Bedford Forrest and His Critter Company.* Nashville: J. S. Sanders & Co., 1992.

McLemore, Richard. *A History of Mississippi.* Hattiesburg: University & College Press of Mississippi, 1973.

McWilliams, Trista R. *Iberville's Gulf Journals.* Tuscaloosa: University of Alabama Press, 1981.

Miles, Jim. *A River Unvexed.* Nashville: Rutlege Hill Press, 1987.

Mississippi: The WPA Guide to the Magnolia State. Jackson: University Press of Mississippi, 1938.

Morris, Willie. *The Ghosts of Medgar Evers.* New York: Random House, 1998.

——. *Good Ole Boy: A Delta Boyhood.* Oxford, Miss.: Yoknapatawpha Press, 1986.

Newton, Caroline. *Meet Mississippi.* Tomball, Tex.: Strode Publishers, 1976.

Percy, William A. *The Collected Poems of William Alexander Percy.* New York: Alfred A. Knopf, 1950.

——. *Lanterns on the Levee.* Baton Rouge: Louisiana State University Press, 1978

Sansing, David. *Mississippi: Its People and Culture.* Minneapolis: T. S. Denson & Co., 1981.

——. *The University of Mississippi: A Sesquicentennial History.* Jackson: University Press of Mississippi, 1999.

Saxon, Lyle. *Father Mississippi.* New York: The Century Company, 1927.

Sibley, Mario. *Mississippi Off the Beaten Path.* Old Saybrook, Ct.: The Globe Pequot Press, 1997.

Smith, Frank. *The Yazoo River.* Jackson: University Press of Mississippi, 1988.

Stall, Gaspar J. ("Buddy"). *Buddy Stall's New Orleans.* Gretna, La.: Pelican Publishing Company, 1990.

Sugg, Redding S., Jr. *The Horn Island Logs of Walter Inglis Anderson.* Jackson: University Press of Mississippi, 1985.

Thigpen, Samuel. *Pearl River: Highway to Glory Land.* Kingsport, Tenn.: Kingsport Press, 1965.

Twain, Mark *Life on the Mississippi.* Cutchogue, N.Y.: Buccaneer Books, 1996.

Walton, Anthony. *Mississippi.* New York: Vintage Books, 1996.

Ward, Geoffry C. *The Civil War: An Illustrated History.* New York: Alfred A. Knopf, 1990.

Wells, Dean Faulkner. *Mississippi Heroes.* Jackson: University Press of Mississippi, 1980.

Wells, Mary Ann. *A History Lover's Guide to Mississippi.* Brandon, Miss.: Quail Ridge Press, 1988.

Wills, Brian. *A Battle from the Start: The Life of Nathan Bedford Forrest.* New York: HarperPerennial, 1992.

Windham, Kathryn Tucker. *13 Mississippi Ghosts.* Tuscaloosa: University of Alabama Press, 1988.

NEWSPAPERS

Biloxi Sun Herald

Chicago Tribune

Greenville Delta Democrat Times

Greenwood Commonwealth

Hattiesburg American

Jackson Clarion-Ledger

Jackson Daily News

Jackson Weekly Pilot

Laurel-Leader Call

Leland Progress

Lexington Advertiser

Louisville Focus

Memphis Commercial Appeal

Metro Business Review

Miami Herald

Mississippi Free Trader

Mississippi Sun

Natchez Daily Courier

Natchez Democrat

Northside Sun

Pascagoula Mississippi Press

Press Register

Starkville Daily News

Times-Leader

Vicksburg Sunday Post

Wall Street Journal

PERIODICALS AND OTHER SOURCES

Amazon.com

Frontier Times

Guard Detail: A Chronicle of the Mississippi National Guard

Journal of Chickasaw History

Journal of Mississippi History

Mississippi Lawyer Magazine

Mississippi Magazine

The Oxford American

University of Mississippi Law Journal

ABOUT THE AUTHOR

Jim Fraiser is the Director of Legal Defense for the Mississippi Band of Choctaw Indians and also teaches creative-writing courses at Millsaps College. He serves as the contributing editor and photographer for the *Metro Business Review* and is a frequent free-lance contributor to numerous newspapers and magazines, including the *Jackson Clarion-Ledger, Greenwood Commonwealth,* and *Biloxi Sun Herald. Mississippi River Country Tales* is his third book, following the critically acclaimed Southern novel, *Shadow Seed.*